Wild Turkeys: Hunting and Watching

by John J. Mettler Jr., DVM

**STOREY
BOOKS**

North Adams, Massachusetts

The mission of Storey Publishing is to serve our customers by publishing practical information that encourages personal independence in harmony with the environment.

Edited by Bill Overstreet, Elizabeth McHale, and Janet Lape
Cover design by Rob Johnson, Johnson Design
Cover illustration by Jack Mesick
Text design by Cindy McFarland
Text production by Eileen M. Clawson
Illustrations by Jack Mesick
Photograph on page 43 by Jon Reis Photography, provided by Ithaca Gun Co.; on page 44 provided by Mossberg & Sons, Inc.; and on page 132 by Cindy McFarland; all other photographs by Elinor Mettler
Map on page 7 provided by the National Wild Turkey Federation
Indexed by Susan Olason, Indexes and Knowledge Maps

Storey Books are available for special premium and promotional uses and for customized editions. For further information, please call Storey's Custom Publishing Department at 1-800-793-9396.

Printed in the United States by R.R. Donnelley
10 9 8 7 6 5 4 3

Library of Congress Cataloging-in-Publication Data

Mettler, John J., 1923–
    Wild turkeys : hunting and watching / by John J. Mettler Jr.
        p.   cm.
    Includes index.
    ISBN 1-58017-069-2 (alk. paper)
    1. Turkey hunting. 2. Wild turkey. 3. Cookery (Turkey) 4. Wild turkey—Collection and preservation.
    SK325.T8M48 1998
    799.2'4645—DC21   98-6392
                                                                        CIP

DEDICATION

To Joe, my grandson and hunting buddy,
with the wish that all my grandchildren
will enjoy wildlife throughout their lifetimes

ACKNOWLEDGEMENTS

I would like to thank Dr. Alan Peterson
for his expert review and advice, and
Janet Lape, who guided this book to its publication.

CONTENTS

Preface

Hunting the wild turkey in spring is as different from hunting other game as fly-fishing for trout on the Battenkill or Big Blackfoot River is different from dangling a worm in front of a bluegill over its spring nest. Any time of year the wild turkey can be a worthy opponent, a challenge to hunt. Unlike fly fishermen, however, who may use barbless hooks and release fish they do not wish to eat, turkey hunters (unless they're skilled photographers) must kill their prizes.

The wild turkey, once nearly extinct in North America, has seen a dramatic population increase within the past twenty years. In states and provinces where hunting is legal, hunter numbers have increased 8 to 10 percent per year. This book is written as a commonsense reference for those interested in hunting wild turkeys, those who just want to learn more about the birds, and those who want to make better use of those that they kill.

I will first explore the mystique of wild turkey hunting, not just from my own experience but also from that of other men and women who have discovered the sheer fascination of trying to outwit this grand bird. Later I'll discuss how to preserve evidence of your well-earned trophy, such as tails, beards, and spurs, and how to photograph both live and dead birds.

Like the trout, the wild turkey is valued for its delicious meat, but too much good wild turkey meat goes to waste because many lack information on proper handling of the carcass after killing. To provide simple, concise directions on how to handle, dress, store, and prepare turkey for the table is thus another objective of this book.

I hope the following pages will pique your curiosity enough so that you go into the field and learn by experience about America's Noble Game Bird.

Prologue

Far up on the ridge where the first blue-gray hint of daylight glows, the garbled gobble echoes, and your heart sinks. "Too late," you mutter to yourself. It is only 4:45 A.M. but with a full moon setting behind you, the woods are already light enough that you can find your way without a flashlight. What to do? Settle down here where there are a few red oaks with bases big enough to shield your back and make a setup? Or climb on, close to the top of the knob where you thought, while listening last evening, there must be a really big tom?

The sudden "rat tat tat" mating call of a woodpecker, like the hinge on an ancient, rusty barnyard gate, startles you so badly that you jump. Then, seconds apart, to your left and right, two more high-pitched gobbles help you make up your mind: "Set up right here," and the sooner the better.

Sitting with your back to the oak, in full camouflage, including mask and gloves, you feel comfortable and invisible, yet boxed in by darkness. The fluttering of wings just overhead startles you again, and you think of October mornings in the swamp when the red-winged blackbirds almost brushed your head as they flitted through the alders you were hiding under. Now a third and yet a fourth gobble sound nearby, echoing the deep roar of the first one you heard from up on the knob.

Way down the valley geese cry, on the state road a diesel blats, and the gobblers challenge. The unmistakable sound of a milking machine vacuum pump breaks the silence, and your mind wanders to opening day of deer seasons of your youth on this same hillside, when the bell-like sound of milk can lids being hammered off used to ring.

The soft "chur chur chur" tree call of a hen almost over your head breaks your nostalgic reverie. You try to remember to control the duck hunter instinct that tells you to use your call, the deer hunter instinct that tells you to stand up. You are a spring turkey hunter now, and anything you do by instinct will probably be wrong. The fluttering of small birds increases, as do bird calls that you never heard in fall hunting. You vow you are going to memorize them, and try to identify them to record in your journal.

Thinking of your journal, you remember the entry after your first spring hunt. "Out of woods 6:30 A.M. nice jake, four inch beard, twelve pounds. Turkey no challenge for this old hunter." Since then you have hunted three years without a spring bird and made so many mistakes you are ashamed to admit them to other hunters — but you've learned from those mistakes, and also learned to love the spring woods, with their new sounds, sights, and fragrances.

Your excitement mounts as you hear wing movements in the direction of the tree where you heard the hen's tree call. Soon you hear the unmistakable sound of her flapping, sailing down, then landing with a thud. Off to your right you catch both sight and sound as another bird leaves its tree. Is this going to be a repeat of your first year? You have decided that this is the year you are going to carry a bragging-size bird out of the woods, one you can be proud of. No yearling jake for you. You tell yourself to focus, concentrate on that big tom up on the knob. You almost feel as though you can will him down.

The hen seems to be scratching and feeding, but not calling as you wish she would. Is it time to call? With your slate call you give a soft little "scree scree scree." It is answered immediately from high on the knob, but all is silence from the two birds at your level. Twice more what seems to be the same gobbler calls, each time closer. You repeat a plaintive "scree scree scree" and put down your slate. You see dark shadows moving, to both your right and your left — probably the jakes, silent for fear of the boss gobbler. Then your heart pounds as you hear the rushing-air sound that can only be a mature gobbler inflating himself. You freeze and wish you could give a soft call from your mouth, but you're afraid to try. He must know where you are, but so do those apparent jakes out there in the still-shadowy woods. Where is the hen? You hope she doesn't come over to investigate.

Suddenly you realize that although you have your shotgun across your knee, it is pointing the wrong way: To raise it, you must swing it to the direction where the tom is apparently strutting just out of sight. And moving the shotgun will give you away. Time seems to stand still. You wish you could mouth-call. You try the next best thing, your tiny plunger box call on the ground under your right hand. Your hand shakes as you give three soft squeaks.

You forgot the hen. Suddenly she is there, twelve feet away, craning her neck to see where the sound came from. She circles you at that twelve-foot radius and on the second round says "puck!" and "puck! puck!" Then she leaves in a straight line, saying "puck! puck! puck!" for all to hear.

The woods are suddenly silent, until a towhee starts to scold you, "chewink chewink" — or as a schoolyard tease might say, "Ya ya, you struck out again." The towhee leaves, the little birds start to sing again, and you take more notice of them. A tiny yellow-throated one you have never seen before is only feet away from your face. He seems to be talking to you, saying, "Don't feel bad, look and listen to all the beauty around you."

Then the clear, beautiful, flutelike song of the hermit thrush comes from within a shadblow in bloom twenty feet away. The beauty of the spring woods and a sip of coffee from your thermos raise your spirits; you are almost glad you didn't get that tom and end your season so abruptly. Far off you hear a gobble. You pick up your gear, sling your gun on your shoulder, and move slowly in that direction.

Before you begin to hunt wild turkeys, learn all you can about them: Attend seminars, listen to calling tapes, watch videotapes, ask questions of experienced hunters, and observe turkeys in their natural environment. In most types of hunting, the hunt is more important than the kill. This is particularly true in wild turkey hunting. For this reason, and the fact that turkey hunters are made, not born, you must get out and experience hunting to really learn. It is my hope that this book will teach you what others had to learn by mistake, opening your life to hours and days of rewarding experience.

History of the Wild Turkey

Sitting under a hemlock tree, trying to keep dry while deer hunting on a drizzly November day more than thirty years ago, I thought, "I must have dozed and dreamed I heard turkeys." Once I was fully awake, I again heard the "churrup churrip" clearly, unmistakably turkey talk, but in the half light of the hemlock swamp I could see nothing. I had read in the *New York State Conservationist* that wild turkeys were going to be released, but had heard of none in our local area. Still, these were turkey sounds, similar to those I was used to hearing at the Berkshire Sheep and Turkey Farm, a veterinary client of mine.

I loved this particular spot. Deer would come in on occasion to bed down, but even if they didn't, there were apt to be ruffed grouse, squirrels, blue jays, chickadees, and other small creatures that ignored me while I watched and enjoyed them. One day while I sat under this very tree, a red-tailed hawk swept in and grabbed a gray squirrel from a limb over my head and was gone in the blink of an eye. But turkeys? Still, what other creature made such a noise?

The sound surrounded me, and then invisibly drifted past. I turned my head to peer at a movement on my left. For the first time in my life I heard the classic turkey warning sound, "puck! puck!" As I turned my head the whole forest floor exploded with the flapping of huge, black birds.

It was dry under the tree so I stayed where I was. After about fifteen minutes, from a distance away I heard another sound I'd never heard before, the "chur chur chur" of the hen calling the flock to assemble.

1

That experience was my first wild turkey lesson. Every subsequent experience with these birds has taught me more and made me realize I still have much to learn.

To this day I marvel at the wild turkey's hearing and eyesight, unmatched by any other game. As so many hunters say, "If turkeys could detect odors as deer do, it would be impossible to get close enough to kill them."

The wild turkey is mentioned often in early American history. Written accounts of Hernando de Soto, the Spaniard who in 1540 explored what is now the central southern United States, tell of "wild turkey and other small game." Accounts of the feast of thanks that the Pilgrims held in 1621 after their first fall harvest mention wild turkey as one of the meats served. The bald eagle was made the national bird by an act of Congress in 1782 over the protest of Benjamin Franklin, who preferred the wild turkey. Franklin considered the eagle a scavenger and "a bird of bad moral character."

More than two hundred years later, former president Jimmy Carter wrote of Franklin's choice in his thoughtful book *An Outdoor Journal:*

> He must have been a good woodsman, because those of us who have gotten to know the wild turkey would certainly agree that its character, clean feeding habits, intelligence, nobility of bearing, uniqueness to America, strong role in our lives since Colonial times, and its inducement for us to preserve some of our most precious habitat, all warrant recognition in a special way.

The journal of Meriwether Lewis, of the Lewis and Clark expedition, lists the game they killed for food on their trip up the Missouri River in 1804 and mentions wild turkey as one of the preferred meats. But as colonization pushed westward, the clearing of the land and the harvesting of birds for food reduced turkey numbers to thirty thousand a hundred years ago. The only birds left were in the most inaccessible areas.

By 1920 wild turkeys were found in small numbers in only eighteen states, and were extinct in the other thirty.

Origin of the Domestic Turkey

Our tradition of turkey for Thanksgiving dinner has, over the years, spawned domestic turkey production that increases each year. The 1950 edition of *The Columbia Encyclopedia* stated that turkeys were raised mainly for Thanksgiving and Christmas holiday dinners. It also stated that the wild turkey was extinct north of Pennsylvania and in Canada.

Today turkey meat — low in fat, rich in protein, and competitively priced — is available year-round in markets, not just as frozen or fresh and ready to roast, but also as turkey ham, turkey sausage, turkey bacon, and boned breasts, both fresh and smoked. Gourmet restaurants and markets sell at a premium price farm-raised "wild" and "free-range" turkey. But where did this all start?

An Uncertain History

The Latin name for the turkey, *Meleagris gallopavo*, is used for both domestic and wild varieties. A related bird, *Agriocharis ocellata*, or the ocellated wild turkey, was found by Spanish explorers in Mexico and Central America in the sixteenth century. This bird had been domesticated by the Native Americans, and there was apparently a large wild population as well. Some of the domestic ocellated birds were taken to Europe, and perhaps even some *M. gallopavo*. Some sources say that Columbus took turkeys back with him in the fifteenth century. At any rate, by the time the Pilgrims came to North America they were already familiar with the "turkey," a domestic bird in the British Isles and mainland Europe.

We can only guess why this North American bird was called the turkey. Perhaps the birds were first taken to Turkey (a term that once referred to the entire eastern Mediterranean) before arriving in Europe and the British Isles. Another theory I have often heard but cannot verify is that the bald, red-white-and-blue head of the turkey reminded Europeans of turbaned people from the area they referred to as Turkey.

Differences between Wild and Domestic Turkeys

The physical differences between wild and domestic turkeys are vast. You have only to compare a modern supermarket oven-ready bird to a dressed wild bird to see the difference. Despite the difference in shape, however,

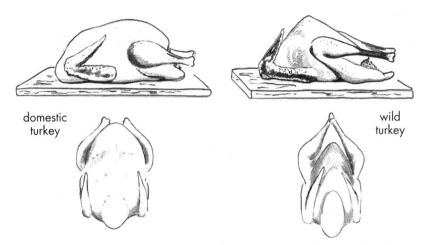

domestic
turkey

wild
turkey

Despite the difference in appearance, the wild bird on the right with its lighter bone has almost as much edible meat per pound of gross weight as the domestic bird on the left.

there isn't, as you might expect, much difference in the "bottom line" — the amount of meat per pound of gross carcass weight.

My grandson Joe Bosnick completed a sixth-grade science project on the differences between domestic and wild turkeys. Joe removed the soft tissue from the bones of two four-month-old turkeys, one wild and one domestic. He measured length, circumference, and marrow space in the long bones, from both the wing and the leg, in each bird. The ratio of length to circumference confirmed that the domestic bird has a much thicker, heavier bone in proportion to its length. The mounted bones

The graceful appearance of the long, slim wishbone of the wild turkey is a good example of the differences between the wild and domestic strains of Meleagris gallopavo.

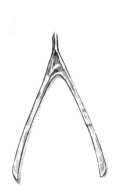

domestic turkey   wild turkey

show this difference at a glance. Just comparing the wishbone of a mature male wild turkey to that of a domestic points out the difference in their conformation.

What it all amounts to is that with its light, strong, slim bones the wild turkey can fly, it can run faster than the domestic turkey, and yet it has more lean muscle in proportion to its weight.

In developing the domestic turkey into a very efficient meat producer, some things had to be sacrificed. One of these is natural breeding — made almost impossible by the shape of their bodies and their short legs. On commercial turkey breeding farms, hens are inseminated artificially anyway, so this is really not a problem.

Attempts to Reintroduce the Wild Turkey

In western Massachusetts during the late 1950s some pen-raised wild turkeys were turned loose in one of the wildest, most remote parts of the Berkshire Hills. Within a few weeks they became part of the scenery. On a summer evening people would drive up the "figure S" in Mount Washington to see the "wild" turkeys standing along the road, waiting for a handout of corn.

That fall a "wild" teenager caught one on a bet and brought it home. Not wanting any more pets to feed, the boy's mother had him kill and dress the turkey for a family meal. She complained that the meat was so fatty that it really wasn't fit to eat. For years after in this area, the food quality of wild turkeys was in question.

Since all domestic turkeys originated from wild strains, it seemed to game biologists in the 1930s that the process could be reversed and a wild strain could be developed from domestic birds.

This thinking may have stemmed from the great success of ring-necked pheasant farms during the same period. Pheasant eggs could be collected from penned hens, incubated artificially or under a chicken hen, and the resulting chicks released to the wild either at a few weeks of age or at any time after that. The released birds not only survived, but also assumed all the wariness and self-preservation of their wild ancestors.

Initial Failures

With *M. gallopavo*, this didn't work. Maybe the domestic turkey was too smart, or perhaps it wasn't smart enough to go out and catch bugs and scratch for acorns. Birds turned loose after being pen raised either starved, were caught by predators, or, more typically, found a kind-hearted country dweller to feed them.

Even where true wild birds were started in pens and then released, the results were dismal. If predators or starvation didn't kill them, disease did. The National Wild Turkey Federation reported: "Raising and releasing pen-raised birds actually slowed down the comeback of the wild turkey by two decades."

The initial problems in reintroducing the wild turkey may be explained today by what we know about "imprinting" — that is, what an animal or bird learns during its first few hours of life. During the first four days of a turkey poult's life, it lives from its yolk reserve while it learns to catch insects that supply protein for rapid growth. If during those first few days it learns to eat human-supplied food, this is apparently what it will rely on for the rest of its life.

Subsequent Successes

In the late 1940s trapping and release of wild birds was tried. Walk-in, drop-door traps were used first, but were good for only a bird or two at a time. In the 1950s and from then on, nets thrown first by cannon and later by rockets were used to capture up to twenty birds at a time. Transport boxes specifically made for individual birds were developed and are still distributed by the National Wild Turkey Federation to state game authorities, in order to safely transport birds to a neighboring state or area where "seeding" is needed.

The federation has reported that a release of fifteen birds (three gobblers and twelve hens) in an area with appropriate habitat may yield four hundred birds in five years. The goal of the federation, in cooperation with state wildlife agencies, is to restore wild turkeys to all remaining unoccupied habitat in the United States by the year 2000.

The results of the past forty years of wild turkey reintroductions have been nothing less than amazing. Wildlife agencies and the National Wild Turkey Federation can be proud of the results. Thousands of unnamed individuals can be proud, too. Although practically extinct in 1920, wild turkeys number close to five million today.

Not only have wild turkey numbers increased dramatically, but so has their distribution. Wild turkeys in viable hunting numbers now inhabit all of the lower forty-eight states, along with Hawaii and southern Canada. I can't tell you the whole story here, but what has happened in New York state and in Idaho are good examples of it.

New York. The last recorded sightings of native wild turkeys in New York state, which had one of the largest wild turkey populations in Colonial times, was in 1844. In the late 1940s a few wild birds from Pennsylvania moved into the extreme southwestern part of the state. By 1957 they seemed well established in this small area. That same year the New York State Department of Environmental Conservation began relocating wild birds to areas in the state capable of sustaining populations. Today, New York state has more than two hundred thousand wild turkeys, with the population growing every year.

Idaho. In Idaho, which never had a native population of wild turkeys, there are more than twenty thousand wild turkeys today. Three subspecies have been introduced: the Merriam's, the Rio Grande, and the Eastern. The Merriam's wild turkey was the first released, in the 1960s, and has been the most successful in Idaho's mountainous woodlands.

In 1982 the Rio Grande wild turkey was introduced into riparian (streamside) areas along the Payette, Snake, and Weiser Rivers. There is

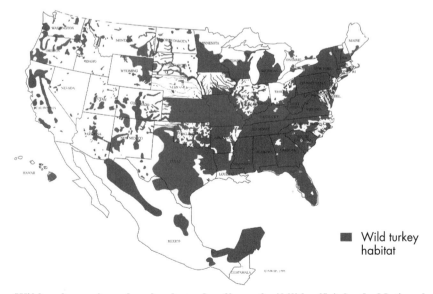

Wild turkeys exist today thanks to the efforts of wildlife officials, the National Wild Turkey Federation, and people like former President Jimmy Carter.

additional similar unoccupied habitat available, and more Rio Grandes will be released.

Near the Dworshak Reservoir, Eastern-strain wild turkeys have been introduced on an experimental basis. The Easterns are larger birds and thus more desirable, but further observation will be needed to determine whether more will be introduced.

The Promise of Reintroduction

A brochure from the Idaho Department of Fish and Game states that "Idaho's wild turkey hunting is increasing in popularity with each passing year. In fact, wild turkey hunting is the fastest growing form of hunting in the U. S. today."

It is interesting to note that aside from Missouri (with 380,000 birds) and Texas (with 600,000), the states with the largest populations of wild turkeys take in the Appalachians — from New York and Pennsylvania to Georgia, Mississippi, and Alabama. I believe that having officials sincerely willing to promote huntable wildlife is the most important factor in these great numbers.

As I think back to that drizzly day when I heard wild turkey talk for the first time so many years ago, I realize that people with ideas and ideals, helped by public and private support, can accomplish almost anything.

THE OCELLATED TURKEY

The ocellated turkey is not a member of the bearded turkey group, *Meleagris gallopavo,* but one of a kind, the *Agriocharis ocellata.* I mention it here because there have been some stories about it in hunting publications.

The ocellated turkey is said to be a beautiful bird, somewhat resembling the bearded turkey but without a beard. It is a bit smaller than the wild turkey and does not gobble. Its spurs are more developed than the wild turkey's.

Ocellated turkeys, both wild and domestic, are found on the Yucatán Peninsula of Mexico and in some Central American jungle areas.

Appearance, Distribution, and Habitat

I live in a house surrounded by a small wood that extends through farm-land connecting it to hardwood-covered hills, and the sight of almost any wild animal or bird doesn't normally surprise me. Pulling into my drive at noon one early-June day I stopped to let a small hen turkey cross, then waited for her to get back into wooded cover. Instead she deliber-ately walked along the drive, heading into a patch of lawn bordered by beds of phlox and irises not more than one hundred fifty feet from the house. Much to my surprise, behind her, out of the woods, came her brood, twelve in all, no larger than robins.

Watching the poults, I took my eyes off her for a second, and when I looked back she had completely vanished. Then, like a fade-out in a movie, the poults disappeared into the iris bed.

With my camera on the seat of the car, the temptation to quietly get out and try to take a picture of one of these tiny birds in hiding was more than I could resist. I was sure that the hen had gone beyond the irises into the thick woods, and that the poults would stay hidden until I left and she called them.

Walking slowly and softly on the grass of the lawn, I reached the iris bed and peered in. No poults were visible. Circling the bed, I kept look-ing for poults but could see nothing among the ten-inch-high leaves.

I backed away from the irises and squatted down to peer into the bed from the side. Then, not five feet away, I spotted the head and neck of the hen, blending almost perfectly with the stalks of unopened iris buds.

Slowly raising the camera, I tried to focus on this remarkable feat of camouflage, only to have the hen stand up and slowly, deliberately, walk

Until the little hen moved, her head seemed to be just another iris bud.

off into the woods. Again I peered into the irises trying to spot even one of the poults. From the woods I heard "puck! puck!" Immediately after, tiny blurs of dark russet brown exploded from the iris bed and, like miniature jets, flew off in all directions.

My guilt was immense. Why had I disturbed this poor mother and her brood? She was already thin and tired from her four weeks of sitting nearly twenty-four hours a day on her eggs, she had brought forth twelve healthy babies, and now they were scattered to the wind. I, of all people, should have known better! I was sure the neighbor's cats would dine on young turkeys by evening.

Half an hour later, sitting gloomily after finishing my lunch, I heard from the woods, between the road and the iris bed, "churrup churrip," as the hen called in her invisible brood.

Two days later at daybreak, twelve poults fed on my back lawn while their mother watched from some brush in the horse pasture.

The wild turkey became extinct in much of the United States and Canada due to indiscriminate hunting and loss of habitat. Considering that the wild turkey did survive in some areas where habitat permitted it seclusion and food, you might conclude that habitat preservation is more important than hunting regulations for their survival.

Knowing Where They Live

Sixty years ago there would have been no place for a hen turkey to hide her brood where my house stands. My grove of sugar maples, locusts, and wild cherries stands where corn, grain, and hay were grown from the early 1700s until the mid-1930s. The fifty-foot-wide strips of oak, elm, ash, and wild cherry trees connecting my woods to the hardwood ridges were fencerows, trimmed of every weed and blade of grass at least once a year. The hardwood ridges were covered with trees sixty years ago, but the trees were only thirty years old, having come in to replace the American chestnuts, dead from blight, and the oaks cut for charcoal for iron smelting until 1902. The small two-acre horse pasture had been part of a seventeen-acre cow pasture until forty years ago, when it was abandoned and allowed to grow up to ash, poplar, alder, buckleberry, and other small brushy shrubs that hide all sorts of creatures, from mice to deer, and from hummingbirds to wild turkeys.

The turkeys that live in close proximity to my residence seem to have adapted nicely to civilization without losing their wild nature. During summer they appear almost tame, yet months before Orion, the hunter, appears in the winter sky they are no longer seen close to houses; they've headed for the hardwood and fir ridges for cover and food. We only see them in the open, on the edges of fields that border woods as they feed on clover, alfalfa, insects, and grains. They have completely reverted to the wildness of their ancestors.

There are species of birds, mammals, reptiles, and fish that are not hunted but that have become extinct or nearly so because of loss of habitat. But what about birds and mammals, such as the Canada goose and the white-tailed deer, that have not only adapted to changes in habitat but have proliferated — so much so that they have become a nuisance in some areas?

As a veterinarian I am well aware that each species is different and must be handled in the way best suited to its particular needs. With this in mind, those of us who want to enjoy wild turkeys by watching, photographing, and/or hunting must rely on the experts — state and provincial game authorities, college and university game researchers, and the National Wild Turkey Federation — to balance hunting regulations against habitat availability, thereby promoting a viable population of really wild, wild turkeys.

The appendix on page 157 lists hunting seasons in the various states and provinces. All states except Alaska have turkey hunting seasons, as does Ontario, Canada. Four well-known strains of turkey are found; some states have more than one strain.

Eastern Wild Turkey

The Eastern wild turkey and the domestic turkey share, in part, the same Latin name, *Meleagris gallopavo*. Further, the Eastern wild turkey carries the same colored feathers as and, in fact, looks exactly like the turkey that every kindergartner or first-grader has drawn or cut out to paste on the school windows before Thanksgiving.

Physical Appearance. A flock of Eastern wild turkeys seen feeding in a field appears black. If one stands erect and flaps its wings, some white will be visible. A hen turkey crossing the road in front of your car on a sunny day may appear a bit bronze.

Seen moving slowly, from thirty or forty yards, they sometimes appear almost grotesque or ungainly, and certainly not beautiful, with their long necks, bald heads, and long legs. If you see a mature male, or "tom," from a distance "strutting," he looks like a small black bear. From close up, with his body puffed up with air, his feathers ruffled, and his tail spread like a

This strutting tom appears as though he is about to burst.

fan, he looks much more impressive, like the turkey on a calendar.

However, until you shoot an Eastern wild turkey or see one held and turned so the sun shines on his unbelievably beautiful feathers, you cannot really know what one looks like. The back feathers, with a burnished bronze bar across the ends, appear almost unreal, as though the bronze stripe was painted on. As the turkey is turned with the sun shining on him, shades of blue, green, brown, bronze, and black combine to create a natural kaleidoscope.

The feather colors and shades may be preserved by proper handling, but I have never seen a photograph that could capture the true color of an Eastern wild turkey as seen close up in the sunshine.

The live tom's head may appear to have white and sometimes even a shade of blue. The bright red of the head, bulbous wattle, and dangling snood of the tom turkey, particularly in the spring, seems to be known to all, though this color, too, fades shortly after death.

By the time a male turkey is close to one year old, bristlelike specialized feather tissue will have given him a "beard" up to about four inches long. The beard does

The color of the tom's head changes from shades of red to white to blue depending on his mood. The size of his wattle, snood, and beard increases with age.

not grow from where you might expect, but from partway down his breast. It continues to lengthen until it reaches ten inches or so, when it begins to wear off. As the tom grows taller the beard continues to grow and may reach over a foot. In winter, hard crusty snow will wear some of these very long beards down. Unlike actual feathers that are molted (shed) and regrown each year, the beard does not shed but continues to grow.

Some male wild turkeys have two or more beards. A small percentage of hen turkeys has beards. Hens with beards are not as common in some areas as others, but most hunting regulations, instead of saying "male birds only," will say "bearded birds only."

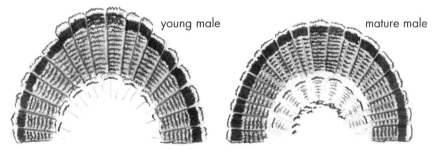

young male   mature male

The center primary feathers of the jake's tail are longer than the rest.

The fan-shaped tail, spread when he is strutting, is the best-known mark of the mature tom. The Eastern wild turkey tom's tail feathers are brown to black with a wide black stripe across near the end; the tips are light brown. Until a young male reaches two years of age, his center tail feathers are longer than the rest. In the mature male all eighteen tail feathers are the same length.

Mature male turkeys have "spurs" — hornlike projections on the posterior part of their legs. A yearling jake Eastern will have quarter-inch spurs, which may grow to one and a half inches if he lives to be three or four. The sharply pointed spurs are used for fighting and can put a nasty wound on a hunter's arm if he or she picks up a dying tom by one leg.

The hen turkey's head is typically blue or almost gray. On occasion she will have a slight pink cast to the bare part of her neck, but no wattle or snood, and none of the bright red of the mature tom.

Eastern wild turkeys are the largest of the so-called big four: the Eastern, Merriam's, Osceola, and Rio Grande strains. A fifth strain, Gould's, is said to be larger. Big tom Easterns may weigh as much as twenty-five pounds prior to dressing, but anything heavier than twenty-one pounds is big.

Weights of more than thirty pounds have been reported, and some people suspect that such large toms had domestic ancestors. I am more inclined to believe the larger birds are the result of good nutrition. Wildlife today secures much of its food supply from farmland. The better the soil and the better the crops are fertilized and cared for, the better the nutrition of the wildlife, leading to larger individuals.

Mature Eastern hens run about ten pounds lighter than their male counterparts. In fall, six-month-old jakes will weigh up to thirteen pounds, and hen poults up to eight. At four months of age the weights will be about five pounds less. With adequate food, the growth of young turkeys from hatching until winter sets in is nothing short of amazing.

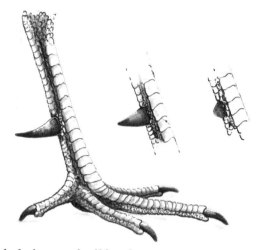

Even with the increased wild turkey population, few toms are around long enough to develop spurs long enough to hang him on a limb.

Habitat. Hardwood ridges with pockets of white pines and hemlocks, surrounded by open pasture or cropland, describes the usual habitat of the Eastern wild turkey.

Due to their will to survive, as their population increases Eastern wild turkeys have been seen in areas that don't fit the above description. As long as they can find food, a secure place to hide, and trees in which to roost to protect themselves from predators, they will adapt. With their varied diet, food is not as much of a problem for them as their need for trees to roost in.

Looking at the map on page 7, you will see that Easterns are found in the Northeast, Southeast, and Midwest from north to south. There are even a few on the coast of Washington state. The states of Idaho, North Dakota, and South Dakota have a few Eastern birds. Some birds are hybrids, which means there is Eastern wild turkey blood in the cross.

For more specific locations of wild turkeys in your home area, contact your state or provincial game authorities. Their addresses may be found in the appendix on page 154.

Rio Grande Wild Turkey

Because the Eastern wild turkey is the most common variety of *M. gallopavo,* my discussion of the Rio Grande's physical characteristics and habitat will highlight only how it differs from its Eastern cousin.

Physical Appearance. The Rio Grande wild turkey strain of the North American bearded turkey, *M. g. intermedia,* appears to be camouflaged for hiding in the sun-drenched surroundings it inhabits. Its tail feathers are tipped with a lighter shade of brown, almost a tan. Viewed from behind, with its light brown lower back feathers and with tail feathers that are lighter than the Eastern's, it blends into the desert.

The Rio Grande hen, viewed from the side or slightly above, has, instead of the dull brown or bronze of the Eastern hen, an almost polished copper hue.

Rios are said to have larger, thicker feet than Easterns, perhaps being better adapted to walking on sand. You might wonder, however, if they developed their large feet for sand, why don't the most northern Eastern birds have large feet to help them walk over the snow?

Rios are slightly smaller than their Eastern cousins, have good beard development, and have somewhat shorter but sharper spurs.

Habitat. There are more Rio Grande wild turkeys than Merriam's or Osceola, but fewer than Eastern. Texas alone has six hundred thousand. If you look at the map on page 7, you will see that there must be more Rio Grande turkeys per square mile in Texas than any other strain in any other area.

Rios are also found in Kansas, Oklahoma, Utah, California, Oregon, and Washington. In addition, there are pockets of Rio population in a few other states in the Southwest. Rio Grande wild turkeys are birds of the desert and of dry open country. Besides food they need trees, such as the live oak, to roost in, and water to drink. Knowing this, after you secure general information from wildlife authorities you can almost pinpoint where you will have to scout to find them in an area by checking a U.S. Geological Survey map.

Texas in particular has many commercial hunting preserves that offer wild turkey hunting. For the beginning hunter or the experienced hunter who does not have a lot of time to scout and hunt, this is a good option.

Merriam's Wild Turkey

Merriam's are often referred to as the Rocky Mountain turkey. Of the eleven or twelve states that have a population of Merriam's, most are in or close to the Rocky Mountains.

Physical Appearance. The most distinctive difference between the Merriam's wild turkey, *M. g. merriami,* and other strains is the white tips to its tail and lower back feathers. Also, black seems to replace most of the brown of the other turkey strains.

The weight of the Merriam's turkey is somewhat less than that of the Eastern. Beards are a bit smaller; spur lengths are about the same as the Eastern.

Habitat. When I think of the Rocky Mountains, where most Merriam's live, I think of aspens and firs, but when I think of turkeys I think of oaks and acorns. Merriam's are found in areas where there are few, if any, oaks. If there are any oaks — even the small Gambel oak, which is similar to but a bit larger than the scrub oak of the eastern mountains — turkeys will find them and use them for roosting sites.

Osceola Wild Turkey

The Osceola, *M. g. osceola,* is said by those who are brave enough to hunt them and skilled enough to have shot one to be the most beautiful of the four main subspecies of *Meleagris gallopavo.*

Physical Appearance. Osceolas have basically the same coloring as the Eastern subspecies, but with less white barring on the wings and far more brilliance of gold and green on their body feathers. Their legs, tails, spurs, and beards are also longer in proportion to the rest of their body. The long legs may help them go through water in the swamps where they live, while their brilliance may be attributed to their being almost a tropical bird.

Instead of the muted, almost dull brown of the Eastern subspecies hen, the Osceola hen has a polished appearance to her light brown feathers.

Although they appear taller than Eastern toms, Osceolas weigh a bit less.

Habitat. Pure Osceolas are found only in southern Florida. Some authorities consider all Florida turkeys as hybrids and refer to them as the "Florida" subspecies. The habitat of the pure Osceola is hardwood swamps and savannas of palmetto grass and live oaks. This also happens to be the habitat of alligators, water moccasins, diamondback rattlesnakes, mosquitoes, gnats, and other creatures not above biting humans. Even if you don't see these other inhabitants when you hunt, knowing they are there can be somewhat distracting.

Within this swamp country, of course, are pasturelands and orange groves where turkeys may come to feed. Still, their main place of residence is the swamp, where they seek out cypresses and live oaks to roost in.

Finding a place to hunt in Florida is difficult if you are not a native. Consulting Florida wildlife authorities as found in the appendix, page 154, may help you find wildlife management areas if you plan far enough ahead. There are also commercially operated hunting camps with guides and all you need for hunting strange territory. Check for advertisements in sporting publications and, again, plan way ahead.

Gould's Wild Turkey

Turkey hunters who have in one year taken all four of the best-known subspecies — Eastern, Osceola, Merriam's, and Rio Grande — are credited with having made a "Grand Slam." For the few hunters who have taken a Gould's in addition to the other four, the term is a "Royal Slam."

If propagation of the Gould's is successful, the "Royal Slam" may become an achievable reality. Even if you're not interested in titles, to hunt and take one of these huge birds would be a thrill.

Physical Appearance. The Gould's wild turkey, *M. g. mexicana,* is the largest of the North American bearded wild turkeys. Gould's are black and white like the Merriam's, with the white brighter and more prominent.

Habitat. Only a few Gould's wild turkeys are found in extreme southwestern New Mexico and southeastern Arizona. Their main range is the arid Sierra Madre Mountains in Mexico.

Attempts are being made to introduce them to portions of the United States too arid for the Merriam's, but efforts are hampered by many factors. One is the rugged area and remoteness of their mountain home. Another is dealing with the regulations of two countries; federal health regulations in the United States require quarantine, which is extremely hard on captured wild birds. A third is that they must be introduced to an area that is free of other subspecies so they can establish a strong enough population to remain pure.

-3-

The Life of the Wild Turkey

For nearly four weeks the twelve light brown, tan, cream, and speckled eggs had moved only when the hen moved. Each movement had been slight, but in the course of twenty-four hours each egg had been turned at least 360 degrees. Today, however, there was movement initiated not by the movements of the hen, but from within. First it was only one, then two, then three. Then there was the sound of a "pip" from the first egg that had moved, as the poult inside forced her beak through the shell.

This first pip was a signal for the hen to start soft, almost inaudible "chirr chirr" calls. In response, there was movement inside several more eggs, and a "pip" from a second.

The first egg soon had a second puncture as the poult turned inside and repeated the process using her beak — specially armed at the tip with a small projection known as the egg tooth, sharp as a grain of sand — to scratch a thin spot in the shell where the beak could be forced through.

The eggs had lain in a depression on the forest

The hen wild turkey leaves her eggs in a pile, ignoring them in an almost casual manner until she starts to set. From then on she is on them twenty-four hours a day, except for a short time when she leaves to get food and water.

floor — you would hardly recognize it as a "nest" — where the hen had deposited them one a day and left. During the days and nights that the eggs had been unattended they had not been discovered by a raccoon, skunk, snake, or any other predator. Freezing nights and cold rain did no harm to the contents, which stayed unchanged from when they were laid, waiting until they would be warmed by the "setting" hen. After laying the twelfth egg she stayed on the nest for nearly four weeks, leaving only for a short time at midday for food and water. Today, the twelfth of May, the twenty-eighth day of incubation, the hatching process had begun.

Late Spring

The flurry of activity in the nest continued for nearly twenty-four hours, with the hen's calls both encouraging and soothing as the twelve poults, after pipping sufficient holes to crack their eggs, each burst from the membrane and shell that surrounded it. The warmth of the hen's body dried the soft down covering of the poults crouching under her.

Early the next day the hen stood and walked a short way from the nest. The poults stood on legs strong enough for their tiny bodies, seemingly confused, leaning against one another. A few soft calls from the hen and they started to follow, as they would for months to come.

Having had no food or drink for two days, the hen headed first for water and then for the edge of the woods, where she could find soft young clover leaves. The poults would not need food for nourishment for another day; they still had in reserve some of the protein from the yolk that had nourished them through their weeks in the egg.

These next two weeks, until they could fly, would be the most dangerous time in the poults' lives. No larger than a sparrow with long legs, they were vulnerable to capture by a host of predators. Insects, the food most suited to them, could best be found in the open field, yet this was the most dangerous place for a young turkey poult to be. Visible from the air, with no place to hide from predators on the ground, their only protection was in being so tiny that they would go unnoticed.

Still, as the sun warmed the field, and as the hen filled her crop with clover leaves, the already sharp eyes of the poults noticed the movement of insects, and the chicks instinctively pecked at them to add protein to their dwindling supply of yolk reserve. Even as she ate, the hen never stopped her soft calling and never let her attention wander from protecting herself as well as her brood.

There would be no going back to the nest for this family. True to their species, they moved slowly but constantly: Eat and move on, eat and move on. They scattered as they hunted insects, but on a signal from the hen they would line up in single-file formation and follow her. Back in the woods toward evening, a call from the hen would cause them to suddenly disperse and vanish.

The poults crowded under the hen for the first few nights, but with their high-protein diet they grew so fast that soon they no longer all fit. It was time then for them to stay on the ground, slightly scattered and hidden, as the hen roosted above.

When the poults were about a week old the hen led them to a field of alfalfa simply teeming with insects. They were busy eating when a young coyote appeared. The hen gave a soft call, which caused the poults to disperse and hide while she, seemingly unconcerned, continued to feed. As the coyote got close she began to move away, dragging one wing, hopping as though not only a wing was broken but a leg as well. The coyote gave chase and was allowed to almost catch her until she was far away from the poults. Taking to the air, the hen flew just off the ground ahead of the coyote until she curved into the woods and alit in a low tree. The coyote watched her hungrily for a few minutes, then lost interest and left, looking for easier game.

A few days later the brood was not so lucky. A feral cat appeared suddenly on the scene and grabbed one of the poults before they even had a chance to hide. Two days later a red fox caught one of the smallest of the poults. That evening an owl swept down on silent wings and flew off with another. The hen, with her remaining nine poults, retraced their path to the field near where the nest had been. Food was not as plentiful here but the area was more remote, with less danger.

The poults had nearly doubled in size in the first two weeks. Their wing feathers, already present as pinfeathers at birth, had developed, and they were able to fly up into a bush or low tree at night while the hen roosted higher.

Summer

About six weeks after this brood was hatched, another hen and brood moved into the area. Instead of one hen and nine poults, now there were two hens and sixteen poults. Able to fly well and roost in larger trees, this new larger flock could feed in wooded areas where there was a good selection of food, from salamanders to blueberries, in addition to the fields with insects, alfalfa, and clover near large trees. They moved each day to a different area, never roosting in the same spot two nights in a row.

The poults did not always listen to the calls of the hens. At times they would go on ahead and appear to be looking for a better supply of grasshoppers, crickets, or ripening grain in farm fields. One day a particularly independent hen poult was out in a field, far away from the rest of the flock, when from far overhead a red-tailed hawk screamed. The poult did not hear her mother's call to freeze and continued to move about. Suddenly she was grabbed by the talons of the redtail and carried aloft to her death. Now, of the original twelve, there were eight.

By the time the poults were four months old, the males were almost as tall as the mother hens and starting to show red about their heads. The flock of two hens and sixteen poults, minus the one that the red-tailed hawk had taken, had now grown to four hens and twenty poults. The latest additions were younger and smaller. Sometimes they would travel and roost as one flock; at other times they would go their separate ways, with the poults following in single file behind their own mothers.

Perhaps because of the lesson from the redtail, or perhaps just from being older, the poults all became more cautious. Unlike Canada geese, which always have ridged lookouts appearing like periscopes, the turkey flock seemed more casual. Yet even when they were feeding, which was most of the time, any movement from any direction, above or around them, got their attention. A poult would give a high-pitched cluck that would alert a hen, which would give a "puck!" to get the flock's attention, and then a "puck! puck!" that sent the whole flock flowing across the field — not walking, not quite running, just sort of floating over the landscape until they disappeared.

Autumn

In fall more broods joined the flock, and their feeding habits changed. Soft mast, wild apples, wild grapes, chokecherries, wintergreen, and partridgeberries all fit into their diet. They still came to the open fields for grasshoppers, crickets, and legumes, such as clover, alfalfa, and trefoil, but seldom came out too far from the protection of the trees. When they went into the fields, if they were undisturbed they usually returned to the woods at the same place they had exited.

Later, hard mast, or acorns — the wild turkey's favorite — would keep them in the woods for days at a time. In addition, there were hickory nuts, hazelnuts, beechnuts, and the seeds that fell from ash trees. Corn from farm fields was also relished, but only if it was near the edge of a field. Unlike pheasants, turkeys seldom go into standing corn.

During this good time of year, with their crops full at roosting time, they might stay in the trees until two hours after daylight.

The flock grew to more than sixty birds, encompassing nine broods and several hens, young and old, without broods. On occasion they would meet another flock, much smaller in number but consisting entirely of male birds, from yearling jakes to mature toms.

When frightened by a large predator, such as a bobcat, fox, or coyote, springing at a poult, or the sudden appearance of a human hunter, the large hen-and-poult flock would fly and run in all directions. When all was quiet again they listened for the call of the hens and regrouped. The poults, too, would call, giving a "kee kee kee" when lost or out of hearing of the hen. Their flocking instinct was so strong that on occasion they would be fooled and shot, called by a hunter imitating a hen or a lost poult. Several, including one of the original brood hatched on May 12, were lost in this way.

On occasion a bobcat, coyote, or fox would be successful, and among those lost was another from the May 12 brood, reducing its number to six. These losses reduced the large flock by several birds, but more broods and individual barren hens joined, increasing the total number to close to a hundred birds.

As late fall came and trees lost their leaves, hemlocks and white pines became the usual roosting places for the flock, where they could see out but felt more hidden than in a bare oak or ash. Then more humans came into the woods. Unlike the one who were dressed in camouflage and killed turkeys, these wore bright orange. Although they were frightening enough to split the turkey flock into many small flocks, after a few days the turkeys found that these orange-clad hunters did them no harm. They were easy to see in the woods, especially when they climbed trees, so the turkeys just kept out of sight as much as possible.

Winter

As so often happens after a productive summer with good weather, winter started early and with a vengeance. Snow fell, and acorns became hard to find. Unlike the deer and the squirrels, which found them easily by smell, the turkey flock had to scratch the snow away to find them by sight. In their wandering the turkeys found that cow manure spread in the fields contained undigested corn. At first they were frightened of the roaring tractor pulling the huge noisy manure spreader, and didn't come into the field until late in the morning, when all seemed quiet. As mast became harder to find in the woods, though, hunger overcame their fear of the machinery. The reunited large flock roosted near where the manure was being spread and waited for the tractor each morning. They would feed on the manure and then go back into the woods to search for acorns, and scratch under the wild cherry and chokecherry trees looking for pits.

When the snow was deepest in winter, the farmer stopped spreading manure and the turkeys had to resort to scrounging anything they could. Buds from poplars and other softwoods, such as black birches, provided food, but it was difficult for the birds to get enough to fill their crops. Windswept cornfields provided some corn, but more seeds from summer grasses. It took a lot of these, too, to fill a crop.

Wet holes, or seeps, in the woods and in old pastures stayed free of snow and provided a few beakfuls of grass and moss for food. Sumac berries, ignored in better times, were relished. Berries from barberry and the tiny bitter apples from hawthorn — ignored like the sumac earlier — gave nourishment too.

Some of the flock overcame their fear enough to go near the farm and search at the trench silo for waste corn. Others even went into the cow shed, where they found leftover corn in the feed bunks.

As the subzero temperatures and deep snow continued, the suffering of the turkey flock became worse. An occasional smaller, weaker bird would die clutching the branch she roosted on, and then, in a day or two, would fall to become a meal for a coyote, fox, or bobcat. One more of the May 12 brood died this way, reducing the remaining birds to five.

When a deep powdery snow fell, some birds never left the roost because they could not walk through it. Staying on the roost conserved their strength. When humans on skis or snowshoes passed under the trees where they were roosting, the turkeys ignored them, but if noisy snowmobiles approached they became frightened and tried to fly away, using up precious energy. Several more birds died.

When the weather warmed a bit during the day and the snow, refreezing, crusted over at night, the surviving birds could walk on the snow and go out to hunt for food.

A winter rain was hard on the birds but also lowered the snow so that they could get to bare ground to search for food. It also enabled the farmer to spread manure again. In addition to natural food, such as hard mast and weed seeds exposed by the thaw, the corn in the manure brought most of the flock through.

Early Spring

By early spring natural wild foods were again found: plants sprouting under the leaves, some acorns, and leftover wild cherry pits. These wild turkeys were survivors and changed their diet to whatever was available. The five remaining poults of the May 12 hatching were now ten and a half months old. The two young jakes, whether by choice or after being driven out by the hens, left with three other jakes and formed a new group. And with small groups of hens of various ages moving on to territory where food was available, the large flock was no more.

The flock of mature toms and the two-year-old jake had split up completely at the first hint of spring, with each finding his own territory. By the middle of March, these males were gobbling from their roosts each morning and strutting at the sight or sound of a hen. The more dominant toms competed to collect a harem of eligible hens, while the younger ones, staying on the fringes, tried to lure an odd hen away.

The three almost-yearling hens, despite the rough winter, had grown and developed so well the summer before that some of them would breed, lay a clutch of eggs, and hatch out a brood. The older, bigger individuals among the flock of yearling jakes, if given the opportunity to mate with a hen, would be able to fertilize her.

So now, a year from the day when the twelve poults of our story, now reduced to five, struggled out of their shells into a dangerous and inhospitable world, the cycle is ready to start over.

ANOTHER PREDATOR

One predator given little mention in the story of the May 12 brood is the great horned owl. This night hunter can kill a full-grown turkey, and turkeys apparently know it. The call of the great horned owl, a deep, resonant "hoo hoohoo hoo hoo" in a tree over your head at daybreak, will make the hair on the back of your neck stand up straight. It will also send a flock of hungry turkeys scurrying over the mountain and into the next valley without a look back.

In order to successfully watch, photograph, or hunt the wild turkey, you must first know what it looks like and where to find it, which I discussed in chapters 1 and 2. Equally important, however, you must know its habits — how it acts, how and what it eats, how it reproduces, how it cares for its young, how long it lives, how it copes with its enemies, and a dozen other perhaps less important, but still interesting facts.

Every time I hunt turkeys, every time I see them during the off-season from my living room window, through my windshield, from cross-country skis, or simply while in the woods on a hike, I learn something new. When another turkey hunter says excitedly, "You know what I saw today?" I listen. Some of what they saw will fill gaps in my knowledge.

Let me now focus on the mating and roosting habits of wild turkeys that I have not already covered, starting with the Eastern strain and then moving on to the main differences that are found in the other major strains.

Mating Behavior

The story of the May 12 brood covers the everyday life of turkeys during their first year. It does not discuss mating details most important to a turkey hunter: how the hen acts when in heat — when she feels the need to be bred by the tom and will accept his advances — and how the tom, the jake, and other turkeys act toward her.

In nature, the hen does not call the tom to her. On the contrary, when a gobbler sounds off, if the hen has the physiological urge to be bred, she

ROLE REVERSAL

As a spring turkey hunter you are attempting to reverse mating roles by bringing the tom to you, the "hen." You may be successful in midmorning in mid-May in the Northeast, because by that time all of the available hens are bred and setting, and the toms are still anxious for more sex. If you sound like a shy young hen, the tom may come to you. Using a decoy may distract his attention from you; all sorts of other aids are useful too. Chapter 5 includes a discussion of calls (page 52) and decoys (page 57).

may answer, but she won't stay where she is — she'll go toward him. When she gets close the tom may become so excited that he goes into a strut.

The strut consists of the tom sucking in air, inflating himself until he literally doubles his size. His feathers are ruffled and his tail fanned out. He drops his wings so that he drags them on the ground, wearing the ends of his wing feathers to needle-sharp points. If you're traveling through turkey country anytime from February on, you may come across evidence of strutting: the tom's tracks and the outrigger trails of his wings.

If given the choice of toms, it is said that the hen will pick the biggest, most vocal available. I'm sure someone has made a study of this. At any rate, when the hen reaches the tom she lowers her rear toward him, and once out of the strut posture he mounts her, forcing her to the ground. She then has to turn her tail up and sideways, exposing her cloaca (a single body opening for urinary, digestive, and reproductive systems). He, at the same time, bends his tail down so that his cloaca touches hers while he infuses semen into her.

Once the two have bred, the sperm in the semen go into the hen's oviduct, where they may remain viable and fertile for up to eight weeks. This is important to know, because any egg produced by the hen for eight weeks after she has been "covered" by a fertile male turkey will be fertile. A hen that is covered in mid-March, lays a clutch of eggs, incubates, and hatches them — only to lose the poults to a fox or bad weather — can nest again before mid-May and bring forth a healthy brood in early June.

After breeding the female, the male turkey leaves the entire reproductive process and care of the young up to the female. Once breeding season is over, the mature toms and yearling jakes flock together, staying completely separate from the hen-and-poult flocks until the next spring.

These all-male flocks are tempting to the fall hunter but, despite claims by some hunters far more skilled than I, it is next to impossible to call them in either before or after breaking up a flock. *The Compact Book of Hunting,* edited by Jim Rikhoff and published in 1964 by J. Lowell Pratt & Co., advises that the only way to get a wild turkey in fall is to study feeding habits and wait nearby. Even today I can find little better advice, other than perhaps using jake or tom decoys.

Roosting Behavior and Strut Zones

A spring turkey hunter needs to know where toms usually roost. Until weather is really warm they will, if possible, pick a pine or hemlock tree near the top of a rise or ridge. As mentioned earlier, the subdominant toms will

ROOSTING ON A FULL CROP

Years ago research on chicken and turkey digestion showed that a crop (the first sac in the avian digestive system) with small amounts of grain will empty in sixty to ninety minutes as the food passes on to the rest of the digestive system. A full crop will not empty for up to eighteen hours. This explains why turkeys that have filled up on food before going to roost will not return to their feeding ground until midmorning. If they go to roost with crops less than full, they will typically visit their feeding ground at daybreak.

---

not be too far away. As the weather warms they leave the fir trees for hardwoods and may even roost at the edge of a wood bordering open fields.

Wherever they roost, they will also have a clearing, a logging road, a patch of pasture, or a long narrow hay field for a strut zone. Early in the season they may not use the strut zone at all, or they may wait until late morning. Late in the season, if hens are scarce they may hit the strut zone directly from their roosts.

During breeding season Eastern toms tend to roost in the same immediate area that they have claimed as their territory. However, if they receive too much hunting pressure they may suddenly leave for a completely new area.

Habit Differences in the Rio Grande

Wild turkeys prefer to roost in oaks, but trees are so scarce in Rio Grande wild turkey country that toms are forced to share their roosting trees with others. In Texas, live oaks are the place to look, but cottonwoods are also used for roosting. Farther north in Rio country there are no oaks, so cottonwoods and sycamores are most apt to serve as roosting areas, with hackberries also used when available.

In the open country inhabited by the Rio Grande wild turkey, strut zones can be anywhere. Once they leave the roost in the morning, birds may travel for miles before settling down.

Habit Differences in the Merriam's

Merriam's wild turkeys like to roost in ponderosa pines on the sides of canyons, and near creek beds. In the northern part of their range, where there are grasslands within the pine forests, they will roost in the pines. Farther east, where there are no pines, they will roost in hardwoods.

Merriam's like to travel, and not alone as the Eastern tom does, but with other toms, jakes, and, of course, hens. Again unlike the Eastern tom, they seem to find a new roosting area each night.

The Gambel oaks in the Merriam's mountain country are not big enough for roosting but do have acorns. Merriam's hens use Gambel thickets for nesting and feeding, so Merriam's toms may be found there also.

Habit Differences in the Osceola

The Osceola wild turkey likes to roost over water in cypresses but will fly to the nearest dry land to strut. The unusual conditions of their habitat make it difficult for hunters who do not have an experienced local guide.

Habit Differences in the Gould's

Gould's turkeys live in drier regions than their smaller Merriam's cousin. While perhaps more secretive and wild, the habits of the Gould's are similar to those of the Merriam's.

THE HARD FACTS OF LIFE

Wild turkeys have the potential to live as long as domestics — until their early teens. However, knowledgeable sources say few live past five years. As in the story of the May 12 brood, more than half the poults hatched don't reach one year of age.

PART II: THE HUNT

The Ethics of Hunting

Growing up on a farm and walking to a one-room school during the 1930s has perhaps given me a little different feeling about hunting than if I had been born fifty years later. Yes, I knew kids in that school who were hugged by their mothers if they shot a squirrel or rabbit, because it meant meat on the table to supplement the cabbage, potatoes, and salt pork that poorer families lived on.

However, every one of those kids loved to hunt as a sport, and they followed the rules. This meant that even if a sitting hen pheasant made an easy shot and a delicious meal, they would not break the rule that you shot only cock pheasants, and in season. They scorned meat hunters, who didn't follow these rules but only killed to feed themselves. Just as scorned were those who killed animals and birds only for "sport" and did not utilize the meat and/or fur.

Boys and girls of my generation were taught that if too many people broke the rules, there wouldn't be any hen pheasants or seed game left to reproduce for the next season. We thrilled at the challenge of outsmarting a gray squirrel, or waiting for a cottontail to stop so we could hit him in the head with a .22 short and not spoil any meat. But when the season closed, we did not hunt.

Young people of my generation raised in the country learned it was proper to hunt and kill game mammals and birds, but we also learned to respect the life of all creatures, wild and domestic. We learned about death and about guns. I can remember as though it were yesterday the first rabbit I shot. One minute he was bounding, escaping; seconds later he was dead, still warm and soft, but dead.

The kids I grew up with learned from this sort of experience the finality of death and the power of guns, lessons you never forget. Beyond this they learned to identify birds, all sorts of other wild animals, trees, berry bushes, wildflowers, and weeds — good ones such as the edible dandelion, yellow dock, and field mushroom, and bad ones such as poison ivy and the deadly death angel mushroom.

When those same kids returned from World War II (minus one or two buried in France or on Saipan), we'd meet in the woods hunting deer or grouse. More than ever, we talked not of the game we shot but of the good feeling we had about being in the woods. A few years later, I might meet one in the woods on a Thanksgiving morning with a son or daughter. The quarry was far less important than telling that child, "When we were kids we used to come up here on this knob and just sit and talk. Once we saw a white weasel catch a mouse right over there by that big white boulder!"

When we were growing up, wild turkeys appeared only in stories about the first Thanksgiving. Pheasants, rabbits, woodcock, and grouse (we called them partridge or "pats") were common. Deer soon became more plentiful, as upland game became scarce. Regardless of the quarry, though, most hunters regarded the hunt as more important than the hunted. To shoot a mammal or bird and not completely use its meat was simply not done — but still, "just being in the woods" was what most hunters considered the reason to hunt.

About the same time that the wild turkey population began to increase, some people began to look into the moral issue of whether it was wrong to kill wild animals for any reason other than to feed a hungry family. To my mind, hunting also feeds a different kind of hunger — the hunger of the inner psyche to be in the woods, to pursue game as our ancestors did for thousands of years.

Moreover, were it not for the hunting-license fees that support the various wildlife conservation agencies, there would be no wild turkeys for people to enjoy, whether they hunt or simply watch. The wild turkey was brought to near-extinction by people hunting for meat and not for sport. Birds were shot from long distances with rifles, caught in baited traps, killed at night on their roosts with no thought of saving hens for the next generation. Conversely, today's wild turkey hunting regulations give the bird the advantage. To bag a wild turkey by following the rules challenges our hunting ability more than any other game that I know of, and yet, thanks to sixty years of modern conservation progress, the opportunity is available to any of us.

The quality of life in the wild is far more important than the quantity. While we often idealize it, life in the wild ends either violently or slowly by starvation and the debilitation of old age. Taking the life of a game species by gunshot or bow and arrow is sudden, and thus not nearly as cruel as nature's own ways. I have no disagreement with people who choose not to hunt, particularly if they also do not consume meat — unless they want me to follow their lead and thereby deprive myself of some of the most satisfying hours of my life, not to mention some wonderful, healthful food.

Clothing, Weapons, and Other Equipment

A flash of light caught my attention. Curious about its origin, I concentrated on where I'd seen it, perhaps three hundred yards ahead. Seconds later it appeared, disappeared, and appeared again as though someone was signaling with a mirror. With the morning sun at my back I should have been able to see a person if someone was there, but all I could see were tree trunks, shale outcroppings, and an occasional small bush with brown leaves.

The flash couldn't be from a discarded glass bottle, since it had moved from where I first saw it. I again tried to determine from past experience what it might be. I had once hunted with a young man who was a deaf mute. Unable to call out or whistle, he had all sorts of other ways of getting other hunters' attention. Flashing a mirror was one that he used, but if he was in the area again I knew he would have contacted me before going into the woods.

The flash would come closer for a few yards or less, then stop and disappear. Thinking back to the favorite stories of my boyhood about the cavalry and Indians in *Colliers* and *The Saturday Evening Post,* I fantasized a possible explanation: "An Indian scout with a shiny gun barrel!" By now, at less than two hundred yards, I could not see a hunter, but the flash continued.

As I watched the on-and-off flash get closer I began to make out the outline of a hunter. My Indian scout idea didn't seem so silly. This person was a good-enough still hunter to qualify as an Indian. Still, no Indian would walk around in the woods in perfect camouflage, carrying a gun with such a shiny barrel.

I pulled my orange hat from my pocket and, waving it, called, "Hello!" He pulled his head netting and hat off and we silently walked toward each other.

Remembering that I still had my face covering on, I started to remove it when he said, "Hi, Doc. Your face may have changed these last forty years but your voice hasn't."

I asked, "George?"

"Right," he replied. "Last time we were up on this ridge we were following your old Red Bone when he took off on a bobcat that jumped tree, remember?"

"The turkeys we had at Berkshire Sheep and Turkey Farm back then were easier to fool than these wild ones are."

George went on, "I do pretty well with the wild ones on my place in Virginia, but this morning I've gotten just within sight of two different flocks and then had them just plain disappear before I was close enough to really break them up."

I said, "I saw the flash of your gun barrel three hundred yards away. Thought for a second it was our old hunting buddy Jackie flashing a mirror like he used to. As it kept moving, though, I realized it was a gun barrel. If I could see it, it must be like a strobe light to the turkeys. Still, I couldn't see you until you were right up close here. You sure show your Indian ancestry the way you move in the woods, but don't the Virginia turkeys see the sun shining on your shotgun?"

"Not my shotgun, it's my brother-in-law's Model 3000. He uses it only for pheasants over dogs at the game farm. I have a Remington 870 with a dull-finish barrel down home, but didn't bring it up. I used to have a lot of confidence in your diagnostic ability on our sheep troubles at Berkshire, so even though I was the hunting expert in our coon-chasing days, I'll take your suggestion and get a camouflage sleeve for this barrel, or hunt only on foggy mornings."

There are full-length books describing the proper clothing and arms for hunting wild turkeys. Every hunting magazine is filled with attractive ads describing the latest camouflage and newest shotgun models designed just for wild turkey hunting. It does seem plausible that we should wear a different camouflage design to hunt in early spring, when trees are bare, than later when leaves are green, or in fall when they are red, yellow, and brown. Still, some of the most successful wild turkey hunters you will meet are wearing the same old camouflage, spring and fall, that they have worn for fifteen years, and using the same shotgun they shot their first trophy tom with.

Camouflage pattern and color are not nearly as important as staying perfectly motionless with a solid background, such as a tree, obliterating your outline. A turkey hunter sitting absolutely still in blaze orange camouflaged with a broken black pattern won't be detected by a turkey as quickly as one whose camouflage blends perfectly with the surroundings but moves. You can wear bark and resemble a tree trunk, but tree trunks don't move.

The adaptability of a shotgun to the shooter, its shot pattern, and a dull finish are more important in being able to kill a good bird than its gauge, design, or action.

Before going out and spending a lot of money on clothing and equipment, evaluate what you have on hand. Further, if what is on hand doesn't seem adaptable to turkey hunting, you should talk to other hunters and reliable sporting-goods merchants in the area where you are going to hunt. In this book I can give you some general information, but only a person who has successfully hunted in a particular area can tell you what is best there.

In the next few pages I'll attempt to describe some of what is available in clothing, footwear, accessory equipment, calls, guns, and ammunition. Wherever possible, if I have comments drawn from my own or others' experience, I'll mention them.

Clothing

More important than camouflage are comfort, silence, and safety. The best camouflage in the woods isn't worth a thing if you're uncomfortable and have to move, or if the material of the camouflage makes a noise when moving, no matter how slight.

Undergarments

I'll start with underwear. Cotton next to the skin that will take up perspiration, and will fit well enough so it will not bind or chafe you when you walk, is important. Color should be taken into consideration too, particularly in the second layer. A white or, worse yet, a red turtleneck or Duofold undershirt exposed as you take off your outside camouflage to field dress a bird can be dangerous. Camouflage is available in these articles of clothing, but dull green, forest green, or just plain old G.I. olive drab is safer than red, white, or blue. The same goes for socks, which must fit and be comfortable for walking. For hot-weather hunting, net undershirts in dull colors are available. Net camouflage shirts are also available for hot weather, but you may need insect repellent for protection.

Outerwear

For outer garments, camouflage patterns available besides just the plain military broken pattern in green, tan, brown, and black include the following: Mossy Oak Break-Up, Skyline Apparition, Sniper Fall Brown, Realtree X-tra Grey, Realtree X-tra Brown, Brown A-P Realtree, Advantage, Mossy Oak Treestand, Brown All-Purpose Realtree, Mossy Oak Blaze Treestand — on and on until your mind is confused. In addition to the well-known and advertised patterns, large discount stores carry almost identical copies with different brand names. The camouflage patterns are found in separate trousers, jackets, parkas, bib overalls, rain gear, and coveralls. Combinations of these garments are used, such as a parka over bib overalls or, for warm weather, lightweight shirts and trousers.

One manufacturer of camouflage suggests that a hunter "mix and match" — that is, use a green camouflage top with trousers of the same pattern in brown. This would, in theory, camouflage you sitting on brown, dead leaves against a green leaf background. It sounds like a good idea, but how many different camouflage outfits do you want to invest in?

DON'T MOVE

If you see a camouflage pattern that was highly touted a year ago but this year is being pushed in the surplus sale catalogs, beware. For example, some of the three-dimensional camouflage with movable "leaves" may move realistically in the wind, but if the leaves move on a still morning as you shift your weight or take a deep breath, a turkey won't stand around to find out why.

Perhaps because as a veterinarian I spent my working hours in coveralls, my favorite turkey hunting camouflage is the coverall. For warm days a single-layer soft cotton coverall is excellent. For cold weather, underlayers of wool shirts, turtlenecks, L. L. Bean's wool hunting pants, and Duofold long johns keep me comfortable. Camouflage coveralls with an extra insulating layer, such as Thinsulate, are also available.

If you do buy coveralls, make sure they are easy to put on and take off and large enough to be comfortable when covering extra layers. Remember, layers keep you warm, and may be removed and put in your pack if the day heats up.

Also important in coveralls, bib overalls, and all camouflage clothing is lots and lots of deep, roomy pockets. There never seem to be enough for all the gloves, shells, turkey tags, face netting, calls, and everything else you want to carry. A perhaps unnoticed feature in coverall design, until you go to reach for your truck keys in your trouser pocket, is a slit on the side so you can reach that inside pocket.

MAKE IT SOFT, DULL, AND QUIET

If you end up buying or already have camouflage clothing of the original military pattern, you may find it has a "new-clothes shine" to it. Wash it several times with strong laundry soap and rinse well to remove this shine. Washing will also soften up the fabric, making it less noisy in the woods.

Ideal camouflage blends into the surroundings. A shiny watch strap, the reflection of glasses, or the protruding cuff of a shirt can give a hunter away.

Head and Face Coverings

Camouflage caps and hats are available in all of the many patterns used for jackets, parkas, bib overalls, and the like. But what you wear on your head is perhaps dictated more by whatever type of face covering you use.

More and more, face nets are replacing black makeup. Some of the original face nets were worn over a fedora-like brimmed hat, similar to the netting that beekeepers use. The newer nets fit closely over the face and are more satisfactory. A camouflage cap will fit over most of these. Most sporting-goods stores carry several styles of face coverings. Suppliers include *API Outdoors* and Quaker Boy, among others.

Gloves

Perhaps the most important and most overlooked part of camouflage for wild turkey hunting is hand covering. You can hold your body perfectly still at your setup, but to use any mechanical call and to shoot you must move your hands.

On days when you don't need gloves to keep your hands warm, you could use black makeup on the backs of your hands. It's my opinion, though, that a solid black moving object is probably seen by a turkey almost as readily as a bare hand.

Look in any sporting-goods store or catalog and you will find all sorts of camouflage gloves to match your other camouflage, designed to keep your hands warm as well. Some are listed as shooting gloves; they have a place for you to free your trigger finger. When you have a tom in range and his head goes behind a tree for five seconds, you have enough things to do without worrying about wiggling your finger free of your glove as you raise your gun, release the safety, and take aim. During those five seconds you don't want a hand covering to interfere in any way with the sensitivity of your hands. Try to find gloves that are soft and silent as well as thin enough for you to feel with them on.

Footwear

Most "hunting boots" are designed for cold weather, rugged enough for an elk hunter who has to walk all day long, with "waffle stomper" soles that carry a ton of mud and make a sound similar to the cleats of an Abrams tank on rocks and hard ground.

AGWAY LENDS A HAND

No glove I have ever tried exactly fits my needs as a turkey hunter. The closest thing to it, however, I came upon quite by accident in my local Agway farm store. Along with the white and brown cotton gloves there were some in green, black, and brown camouflage. The cost was less than that of any glove designed for hunting. I didn't really realize how much I liked them until they were washed a few times, losing their sizing "shine" and stiffness. They are the only gloves of any sort that I can feel with as I handle my shotgun. In fact, I have used them with my bow and my deer rifle.

Much to my surprise I found out something else about the cheap cotton gloves. To protect your hands from cold, gloves must not bind, which would restrict circulation. These cotton gloves do not restrict circulation but still fit close enough to allow me to manipulate my shotgun and shoot.

Turkey hunting, however, is seldom done in really cold weather, usually does not involve mountain climbing, may be done in wet places, and demands that everything worn from head to toe be either camouflage or a dull, drab color, as well as silent and comfortable.

For most areas in wild turkey range a soft-soled boot with chain tread, similar to the original L. L. Bean hunting boot but in a drab dull color, that is quiet and doesn't pick up a lot of mud, is ideal. The leather tops on these boots are not that noticeable; they're hidden by your camouflage coveralls or trousers.

Canvas camouflage tops are better yet, but some squeak at each step, or make a scraping sound if you "interfere" — that is, rub one foot against the other.

For wet conditions, olive drab rubber knee boots, such as those made by LaCrosse, are ideal. They are made both insulated and plain. You can walk quietly in these and won't get your feet wet.

IF SNAKES ARE A WORRY

We do have timber rattlers here in the Berkshire and Taconic Hills, and although I've seen the results of their bites on dogs, horses, and cows, I've never heard of a person being bitten. We are more concerned about rabid raccoons than snakes. However, for those who hunt where copperheads, rattlers, or other poisonous snakes are a concern, LaCrosse makes a camouflage, waterproof, seventeen-inch-high "Viper Snake Boot." These, I would say, are designed with turkey hunters in mind.

Choosing the Proper Weapon

The dust from the grinding mill covered everything in the G.L.F. farm store back in September 1952, including Wolverine boots, hardware, fishing gear, guns and ammunition, and the office furniture. In the corner between the owner's rolltop desk and the wall stood what appeared to be an old pump shotgun, dust-covered like everything else. I wouldn't have noticed it except for trying to help the owner, Clyde, find the cat he had asked me to examine. The cat was behind the desk and, as Clyde had told me, his face was "a mess."

Cleaning him up a bit revealed that his bout with a heavily loaded grain wagon had squeezed his head, giving him a pair of bloodshot eyes, a bloody nose, and, most seriously, a lower jawbone split all the way up to the symphysis — that is, where the two sides joined.

When I showed Clyde the problem and moved one side of the poor cat's jaw up while the other went down, I was afraid that he, as many owners, would say, "I've got twelve others. Don't let him suffer, just put him out of the way." Instead he asked, "Can you wire it back together?"

Assuring Clyde that we would try, I put the cat in a box and took him back to our office. As I drove home I remembered the shotgun in the corner. My old Paragon 12-gauge double had developed a nasty habit of either not going off or firing both barrels at once. Considering that I had bought the old gun, very much used, for thirteen dollars seventeen years before, I felt I needed a replacement. But with bill collections going poorly, and paying for a new house and veterinary office, my resources didn't warrant much more than another cheap old double.

The next day when I brought the cat back and showed Clyde the wire job he had asked for, I sneaked a better look at the gun in the corner. "That old pump, is it for sale?" I asked.

Clyde squinted through his thick dust-covered glasses and said, "Oh, that one. It is old, might even be prewar, but never been fired. Forgot it was there, wouldn't have noticed it if we hadn't moved the desk to get this poor cat out."

He pulled the gun out, dusted it off, showed me the tag: FEATHER-LIGHT ITHACA REPEATER, MODEL 37 STANDARD GRADE, 16 GAUGE, CHOKE MODIFIED. "Shoulder it," he said.

I checked to make sure it was empty and raised it to my shoulder. It was love at first sight. "How much?"

"Seventy-five dollars."

Had he said, "Seven hundred fifty," I was so enamored of that gun that I still would have said, "I'll take it!"

That gun and I were made for each other. It was light and easy to carry and fit easily on the rear seat of my practice car, where I could grab it and walk off into a swale or wood to hunt for grouse or pheasants for twenty minutes between calls. With #4 shot it killed ducks in the swamp, and with slugs it killed deer in Massachusetts.

Then came wild turkey hunting. I tried #2 shot, believing the same load I used for geese would be correct. Then I went to #4 shot, and waited until they were so close that I could see their eyes. Aiming at their heads through a low-power scope, I got a few turkeys, but far too many times they were out at least thirty yards, too far to shoot at and kill with the Modified Choke 16.

Then a client told me about the single-shot Mag 10-gauge that Harrington and Richardson made. For two years I hunted turkeys with one and got a couple of birds, but missed more than I killed. I'd used a scope on my deer rifle and my old Featherlight 16-gauge, and the extra range and killing power of the H and R was wasted with my poor shooting.

The February 1985 *Outdoor Life* had an article by Jim Carmichel about Mag 10s in which he praised the Ithaca Mag 10, saying it would bring down geese at eighty yards. By that spring I owned an Ithaca Mag 10 with a scope. The killing range of this big shotgun was not exaggerated in the Carmichel article.

My first love, my old 16-gauge Ithaca Featherlight, cleaned and ready, still stands in the gun closet waiting for the next high cycle of grouse to return. It was an unfortunate day for the feed store cat when he tangled with the feed wagon, but had he not crawled behind that old desk, that Featherlight might still be back there waiting for someone who would really appreciate it.

All the equipment and paraphernalia you use is worthless if a tom comes in close enough to kill and your weapon just can't do the job, either because it is inadequate or because you can't use it properly. Conversely, turkey hunters with a weapon that they have mastered to its greatest efficiency, wearing a minimum of camouflage, and calling without mechanical devices often bag turkeys.

Most turkey hunters use shotguns, but there are circumstances in which a rifle is the proper firearm to use. In addition, some hunters, desiring a greater challenge, use muzzleloaders or bow and arrow.

Choosing the weapon you hunt with is a very personal thing, like choosing a spouse, a friend, a pipe, or a hat. Often something unconscious — seemingly intuition but probably recalled from some experience years ago — makes this shotgun, bow, muzzleloader, or rifle "the right one."

Shotguns

You may have in your gun closet what you always considered the perfect shotgun, as I did my old Featherlight. But you will find out, as I did, that turkey hunting requires a different standard in shotguns. Or you may find that the gun that you killed pheasant, ducks, and geese with for years is in your hands, a first-class turkey killer.

Besides being a gun that you feel comfortable with, a proper turkey shotgun should meet the following requirements:

- It should deliver a dense, tight pattern that will consistently put enough shot in a turkey's head and neck at forty yards to kill it instantly.
- The gun should have a dull finish or camouflage.
- The barrel should be short enough so that the gun can be maneuvered easily in close quarters without hitting brush or overhanging branches.

■ It should be well balanced and light enough for you to hold raised and ready for what might seem like forever, but heavy enough to withstand the reverse wallop that the modern magnum turkey load puts out.

There are trade-offs. My Ithaca Mag 10 weighs eleven pounds, as much as a World War II Garand. Yet despite this, its extra range and killing power and soft recoil make it difficult for me to give it up for a lighter, more easily carried gun.

Remington makes the Model SP-10 Magnum Camo, which is the same as the original Ithaca Mag 10 but with camouflage and a shorter barrel (23 instead of 32 inches). Ithaca no longer makes the Mag 10 but will furnish shorter barrels for the original Mag 10 on special order.

You can buy a 3-inch 12-gauge from Remington, the Model 11-87 SPS-T turkey gun that is like the company's Mag 10 but three pounds lighter. To carry three pounds less you may be sacrificing some killing power and up to ten yards in range.

Perhaps a happy medium would be to buy an Ithaca Model 37 Turkeyslayer in camouflage and 12-gauge 3-inch, which weighs less than seven pounds. This is a pump, and theoretically packs more wallop since it doesn't require energy to autoload.

Remington Model 870 pump shotguns, specially designed for turkey hunting, in black instead of camouflage, and weighing only a few ounces more than the Ithaca Featherlight pump, are also popular.

The Ithaca Featherlight and Remington Model 870 are also available in 3-inch 20-gauge. For women, youths, and even older hunters who desire a shotgun with less recoil, these are alternatives to the 12-gauge. After seeing the patterns that the Remington 20-gauge youth gun delivers and the results on turkeys thirty yards out, I believe that if you recognize its range limit, it is a perfectly satisfactory turkey gun.

Ithaca Model 37 Turkeyslayer, 12-gauge 3", 22"

Mossberg 20-gauge Youth Gun

Mossberg, Ruger, Benelli, Beretta, Stoeger, Savage, Winchester, Browning, and many other reputable manufacturers have shotguns designed for turkey hunting. But any shotgun that meets the aforementioned requirements for a gun to hunt turkeys will be satisfactory in the right hands.

Depend on your local sporting-goods store to offer advice and information. Regardless, you must make the final choice. Don't be afraid to be different. If you have or find a shotgun you are comfortable with and you bring home the turkeys to prove its worth, you need no better argument.

Rifles for Turkey Hunting

The use of rifles for turkey hunting is illegal in most states. However, where they are legal and where terrain makes them more practical than shotguns, the correct caliber and bullet style are important.

Almost any center-fire caliber will kill a turkey, but most with ammunition designed for big game will damage so much meat that they are impractical. The small-caliber rifles — .22 Hornet, .218 Bee, .222, and .223 — are most popular. Single shot, extremely accurate models, such as the Ruger .218 Bee, are thought of as "turkey rifles."

Rim-fire .22-caliber rifles, if used for head shots only, will certainly bring down a turkey. However, the .22 magnum is more practical; it doesn't require a head shot. The longer-range center-fire calibers are more apt to be used.

Ammunition for turkey hunting is usually nonexpanding bullets, which lessen meat damage. At one time I thought the military .223 would be a good turkey load. However, hunting with a friend who was using military rounds to try to shoot woodchucks gave me the impression that the military rounds are not that accurate. Since then I have heard and read that this is true.

A turkey's small kill zone demands accuracy with a rifle. I once sat in a tree stand deer hunting, and watched through my scope a turkey walking by with his head going back and forth; this was enough to convince me that people who shoot turkeys with rifles have to be good shots. Anatomically, the most practical place to hit a turkey with a rifle round to kill him and damage the least meat is very low in the neck, where it joins the body. This is still a tough place to hit, but easier than a head shot.

I must repeat, there are very few areas where rifle hunting for turkeys is legal.

Muzzleloaders for Turkey Hunting

The art and science of black-powder shooting with muzzleloaders is a field all its own. Looking back through American history, you will realize that lots of turkeys were shot before modern arms were developed. However, just as not every modern shotgun is a turkey gun, most muzzleloaders, with their scattershot loads, shot by most people, are not capable of killing a turkey.

Most of the muzzleloaders available today are made for shooting a single ball, like a rifle. Looking through the 1998 edition of *Shooter's Bible*, I find one Classic Turkey Double-Barrel Shotgun made by CVA Black Powder Arm. It is a 12-gauge modified choke, weighs nine pounds, and has a pair of 28-inch barrels with double trigger. It features a ventilated recoil pad, rear sling swivel, and fiberglass ramrod. Looking further, I find that if you don't insist on being authentic and use muzzleloaders with modern choke tubes, you can find turkey-killing muzzleloaders from Cabela's and Thompson Center. Knight Rifles makes a muzzleloader with interchangeable rifle and shotgun barrels with a choke tube, while Dixie Gun Works offers a 10-gauge double-barrel cylinder bore with 30-inch barrels; the latter is said to be an effective turkey killer. (See "Sources," page 162.)

Black-powder enthusiasts tell me that you must experiment with various combinations of shot sizes and weights with various amounts of soft powder and wad types to produce the right combination to kill a turkey, not just knock him down. Small shot, such as #7½, has denser patterns, but some find that with the slow velocity of most muzzleloaders, the small shot won't penetrate bone to reach the spinal cord or brain. Satisfactory penetration is found with #4 shot, but it apparently takes hours of experimentation, and days of sore shoulders, to come up with the exact combination to produce a satisfactory pattern.

I shall not suggest powder charges — that information should be secured from people competent in black-powder usage. The danger of too heavy a powder charge must always be considered.

SCOPES AND SHOTGUNS

When I'd gotten my first scope on a deer rifle years ago, a friend who had successfully used a scope for some time told me, "When you can walk through the woods and pick up a falling leaf through the scope the instant the rifle comes to your shoulder, you are ready to hunt."

Today more and more turkey hunters are putting telescope sights on their shotguns. The wild turkey is North America's biggest game bird, but to kill one you must hit a target smaller than a quail. Most shotgun shooters were brought up to point their weapon, not aim. This works with a pattern thirty inches or more in diameter and a bird the size of a grouse, or a clay pigeon that requires only a few pellets to bring it down. Although one #4 or #6 pellet in a turkey's brain or through the neck vertebrae will kill it, to be sure of securing a hit on these tiny areas you must put several pellets in the head-and-neck region.

The easiest way to achieve this objective is to aim, not point. With turkeys, your first shot is usually your only opportunity and, although your target is still, there is little time to aim. A low-power scope makes this possible. Scopes of 1 to 4 or 5 power seem the most practical, with most hunters using the lower range of 1.5 or 2. This gives you a wide field yet improves your vision and concentration on that vital area, the head and neck.

Most authorities say you should aim at the wattle region of the turkey. My personal experience has taught me to put the crosshairs of my scope on the head. This may be wasting some of the pattern, but I don't end up with a lot of pellets in the breast, which spoils meat and does little to kill the turkey.

It takes a lot more skill and patience to bring a turkey in close enough to kill with a muzzleloader than a modern shotgun, since effective ranges are said to be less than twenty-five yards.

Shotgun Ammunition

With only five ammunition manufacturers selling shotgun shells specifically for turkey hunting, you don't have to be too concerned about your choice. The big three, of course, are Federal, Remington, and Winchester. Fiocchi and Activ, although not as well known, have excellent turkey loads. Usual recommended shot sizes are #4, #5, #6, and even #7½. For big Eastern birds, stay with the largest shot that will give a good pattern.

Of course, there are other brands available with the same specifications as those listed here, but not specifically saying TURKEY LOAD on the box. In addition, if you are shooting a 16-gauge, or even a 28-gauge, you can find shells with enough wallop to kill a turkey under the appropriate conditions. Before going into the field with these, it is even more important to study pattern, range, and limitations.

The importance of pattern. When I talked about muzzleloaders, I mentioned that in order to find the correct combination of shot, black powder, and wad, you have to experiment. The same holds true for the shotgun hunter in search of the right brand and right size of shot to make the best pattern with a particular gun. In addition, you may have to try at least three of the five brands that make turkey loads, and several shot sizes in each brand. Even with boxes of ten shells each, this becomes expensive.

As mentioned earlier, the killing zone on the turkey, our largest game bird, is a smaller target than that on our smallest, the quail. A hole the size of your hand in the shot pattern can lose you a turkey if that hole is where his head and upper neck are. Likewise, shot patterns too widely dispersed might cost you a turkey if only one or two pellets strike the neck-and-head area. True, one #4 shot through a turkey's brain will kill him, but you are safer if half a dozen end up in his head and upper neck, even if none actually hits the tiny brain.

How to determine pattern. You can buy paper targets with turkey heads from your local sporting-goods store, or you can draw your own. These should then be placed on a larger piece of paper, so that you have at least two feet above, below, and on each side of the turkey head. In an area safe to shoot, place a target out twenty-five yards for a 20-gauge, thirty-five for a 12, and forty for a 10. Fire and count the shot holes in the killing zone; then estimate the number in a twenty-inch circle. Are there gaps in the pattern? Is the turkey's head at the center of the circle, and where you were aiming? Is the pattern evenly dense, or is it thin on top or on one side? Now, if everything was satisfactory, move out five yards and repeat.

SHOTGUN AMMUNITION FOR TURKEY HUNTING

Manu-facturer	Brand Name	Shot Type	Gauge	Shell Size	Ounces
Activ	Penetrator	nickel	12	3"	2, 2¼
		plated	12	2¾"	1½, 1¾
Federal	Premier	copper	10, 12	3½"	2¼
	Magnum	plated	12	3"	2
	Turkey		12	3¾"	1⅝
			20	3"	1½
Fiocchi	Magnum	nickel	12	3"	1¾
	Turkey	plated	12	2¾"	1⅜
			20	3"	1¼
Remington	Premier	copper	10, 12	3½"	2¼
	Turkey	plated	12	3"	2
			12	2¾"	1½
			20	3"	1¼
Winchester	Double X	copper	10, 12	3½"	2¼
	Magnum	plated	12	3"	2
	Turkey		12	2¾"	1½
			20	3"	1¼
Winchester	Supreme		12	3½"	2
			12	3"	1¾

Most of the above are available in shot sizes #4, #5, and #6.

Few gun ammunition combinations shot perfect patterns without "holes" big enough to fit around the turkey's vital killing area. You may have to try several brands and shot sizes before you find the perfect one for your gun.

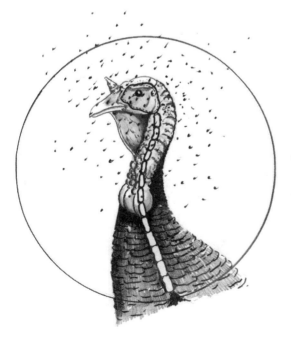

Get to know where your gun shoots so when the long-awaited chance comes you don't "blow" it.

HUNTING WITH NEW TURKEY CHOKES

When fired with shells that are adaptable to their extreme muzzle stricture, the new turkey chokes concentrate the shot spread and put out a tiny, dense pattern. You must do more than point, as you would for a pheasant, grouse, or quail; *you must aim.* You must know where that tiny circle of shot is in relation to your sight or the crosshairs of your scope. You may have to test several different brands and shot sizes to achieve the ultimate with these tight chokes.

Otherwise, if the pattern was poor, try a different shot size or different brand and compare. If the pattern is too high or too far to one side of where you aimed, correct your aim, or adjust your sighting device or scope.

Also important when it comes to killing power is how hard the pellet strikes the bird. It is said that some of the long 12-gauge shells carrying the same weight of shot as that of the 10-gauge just don't have enough powder to put that weight of shot out the long distances. If you have dense patterns with #4 or #5 shot at forty yards, I wouldn't worry about it.

Getting good advice. With a little help from your friends, the job of patterning and selecting the correct ammunition to use in your gun may be easier and less expensive. If you are checking a new gun or patterning a gun for turkey hunting for the first time, ask a friend who is an experienced turkey hunter what brand and shot size he suggests. He may even have a few odd shells of the gauge and shell length for your gun so you can try them first before making a large investment in other brands and shot sizes. Even if a friend's gun is identical to yours, don't be surprised if your gun patterns best with a different brand or shot size. It seems as though life throws us a little curve once in a while to keep things interesting.

If you don't have a turkey hunting friend to ask for advice, in my own experience the Winchester Double X has been the best brand for the guns I use. The XX copper-plated #4 shot in Winchester's 10-gauge 3½-inch Magnum Turkey Loads have patterned well with my old Ithaca Mag 10, the 20-gauge of the same brand, and with my grandson's Remington

COMPUTING DENSITY

To compute density, figure the percentage of shot that hit in a given circle. This requires you to know how many pellets were in the load that you fired. To figure the number of pellets in a shell, multiply the ounces as given on the label on the box of shells by the number of pellets per ounce in the following table:

Shot Size	Pellets per Ounce
7½	350
6	225
5	170
4	135
2	87
BB	50

Using the above table, you will find that a shell of Winchester Mag 10 Double X, or 3-inch 12-gauge with 2¼ ounces of #4 shot, has (2.25 x 135) or approximately 300 pellets. A Winchester 3-inch Mag 20 Double X shell with 1¼ ounces of #4 shot has (1.25 x 135) or approximately 165 pellets. If the Mag 20 put 115 shot holes in a twenty-inch circle at twenty-five yards, you could say that 70 percent of the pellets (115 ÷ 165) were in the circle, which is an acceptable percentage.

Quoting percentages is fine — the numbers let you make comparisons. But the appearance of a dense, even pattern is far more important when it comes to killing turkeys.

Model 870 Mag 20 youth gun. The same shells with #5 shot seem to pattern best in a 12-gauge 3-inch Smith and Wesson pump we have worked with, and a Remington Model 870 12-gauge. Using Federal brand #6 shot patterned best in the Smith and Wesson.

Perhaps the best source of advice as to what brand and shot size are best for your shotgun is the sporting-goods store that sold it to you.

Don't skimp on time or expense patterning. You may hunt for several seasons until the great chance of a bragging-size bird appears. Before you blow the chance because of a blown pattern, spend the extra few dollars to learn which brand and shot size are best for your particular gun.

The largest game bird is the smallest target. To kill outright a pellet must hit the brain or cervical vertebrae. Hits any place else may put birds down, but they will get up and go to die somewhere else.

Calls and Calling

Somewhere I'm sure there is a person who collects turkey calls — not just the antique or historic ones, but a specimen of each and every version sold in the past twenty years. This collector would have to live alone in a huge house, or perhaps have converted an old dairy barn or warehouse roomy enough to hold them all.

Conversely, if you bought or made one of each basic type of call, they would fit in the pockets of one of the new turkey hunting vests that have recently come out.

There are four basic types of calls:

- Friction calls. The most common type, these include box calls and slate, glass, or aluminum disks that need a striker. Most require two hands to operate.
- Wind calls. These resemble wind instruments in the band. They may be operated leaving both your hands free.

■ Percussion calls. These depend on being shaken, rattled, or struck.

■ The human voice. This is considered by many to be the best call available. The problem here is that while some people are blessed with a voice that can imitate any sound they hear, most of us just don't have it and have to end up using a calling device.

I have not included electronic calls, which, to the best of my knowledge, are illegal.

Friction Calls

The basic box call, a box carved out of one piece of wood or made of plastic, usually with a paddle or scraper attached, is the most common type, and can be operated by almost anyone. Lynch and Penn's Woods are but two of literally thousands on the market. Some of these are handmade by skilled craftsmen who turn out only a few each year.

A variation is the little plunger box that can be worked with one hand. Quaker Boy makes one called the Easy Yelper. If I could own only one call, this would be my choice. You don't have to be a skilled caller to bring in toms in spring or recall a flock in fall with this one.

Very popular a few years ago was the slate call, in double and single models. These are disks of slate, about three inches in diameter, set in plastic, that can make a great variety of turkey talk if properly rubbed with a pencil-shaped wooden or plastic striker. Today variations of these in glass, aluminum, and other materials are

box call

plunger box call

slate call

advertised in every hunting publication that is read by turkey hunters. The original slate model can be made to imitate almost every phase of the turkey language. For me, it is best for the early-morning "purr" of the hen waking up in the tree.

Wind Calls

The best known of the wind calls is the diaphragm type, held in the mouth between the teeth and activated by a combination of breath and humming. These rank right up there with the human voice in natural sound, and you don't need to move your hands to operate them. Not everyone can use the original models, however, because many gag on them.

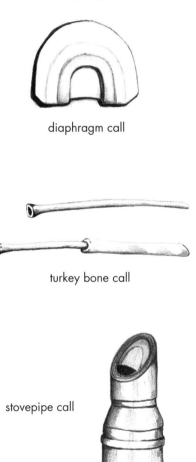

There are many variations of the diaphragm call, with one, two, or three "reeds" — the fine layers of latex that produce the sound. New to the market is a model that is held more forward in the mouth, which may reduce the gagging effect of the originals.

diaphragm call

Another wind call is the turkey bone call made from the radius — the straight wing bone of the turkey. The distal end is cut off, and a hole is drilled in the proximal end in the little cuplike joint surface. This makes it possible to push the marrow out. You can make a sound similar to a hen's yelp by sucking air in from the end you drilled the hole in.

turkey bone call

Recently I have seen advertisements for turkey bone calls that appear to have been made using both the wing bones of the turkey. To me it's more fun to make my own from the wing bone of a wild turkey that I've shot.

stovepipe call

A round metal tube like a miniature stovepipe with a rubber

Locator Calls

Locator calls, used to find where toms are roosting, range all the way from elk buglers to whistles with such a high frequency that humans can't hear them, but turkeys can and will gobble to challenge. More usual are crow, coyote, and owl calls. The owl call is one that I have mastered with my own voice. These may be found in any sporting-goods store that sells turkey hunting supplies.

---

diaphragm stretched over it comprises the so-called stovepipe call. I once won one at a turkey hunting seminar but never felt as though I properly learned to operate it. Other than this I have never known anyone who used one, although I'm sure somewhere there is a hunter who swears by them.

Percussion Calls

There are calls made (similar to some duck calls) that, by shaking, you can use to imitate a tom. For safety's sake, these should only be used for locating toms, and even then caution is advised. If you make a gobble sound someone may take you for a tom turkey and shoot you!

Where to Buy Calls

There are so many versions of calling devices that to list all the suppliers and their particular version of one call or another would be pointless.

Look through the pages of any good publication that features turkey hunting, and read the ads describing calls. Without actually holding a call in your hands and trying it out, however, you can't really decide which is the one or ones to order. So, go next to a good sporting-goods store and try some of the calls for sale. Most stores will let you try all but the kinds, such as the diaphragm, that go in the mouth. And diaphragm calls are cheap enough that you won't feel robbed if you buy one and find you can't work it because of gagging.

If you are a first-time turkey hunter, your first choice should be a good box call, such as a Lynch or a Penn's Woods. Also buy a good instructional calling tape. One of the many available is Skeeter's Practice Tape, which uses the same repetition principal that foreign-language tapes do: "Just listen to the caller, then do your call."

After you have listened to some calling tapes and practiced with the box call, go back to the store and buy a diaphragm and a Quaker Boy Easy Yelper or similar push-button model. Then, after trying some out to see which is easiest for you to operate, buy a slate, glass, or aluminum call.

Of all the diaphragm calls on the market, one in particular has caught my attention. It is a so-called "Lip Call" that doesn't go in the back part of your mouth to gag you. These are sold by Classic Game Calls. (See "Sources," page 162.)

Learning to Call

Sitting on a ridge on a spring morning you are discouraged because nothing is gobbling. You call a few times and then just sit and listen. Down the slope near an open field you hear the call of what you are sure is another hunter. Not only is he a poor caller — his tone, rhythm, and cadence way off — but he shouldn't even be there. You are the only one with permission to hunt this hillside! Now you know why there is nothing gobbling. This intruding amateur with his poor calling has alerted every tom for a mile around.

What to do? If you walk down to him he might shoot at you before you can make yourself known. If you call out to him from up here you'll ruin the rest of your day's hunting.

You decide to go back down to the open field and see if you can locate his vehicle; if the door is unlocked, you can blow the horn and call him back. You know from experience that the sound of a horn doesn't seem to disturb turkeys and might even cause a tom to gobble. If this doesn't work, you'll approach him through the open (with your orange hat and vest) and then call to him.

There is no truck, so you head along the edge of the field, getting more angry every time you hear that stupid call of his. When you get within range of the shotgun he is probably by now pointing toward you, you call out, "Hello, who's hunting in there?" He stops calling but doesn't stand up or answer your question.

You decide to stay in the open where he can see you, walk toward him, and really yell loud this time.

You are prepared to bellow out in rage, "Hello, you in there, come out so I can talk to you!" But before you do you are shocked and embarrassed to see a huge hen turkey take off from exactly where you thought the other hunter was and fly up toward where you had your setup. As though to rub salt in your wounded pride, across the field you spot the black shape of a tom as he scoots into the woods.

If you are a natural mimic and have perfect hearing, you can learn to call well enough to bring in a tom in one or two seasons. If you are like many of us, with hearing problems either inherited or caused by shooting too many times without ear protection, it will take longer. Regardless, every time you go in the woods, either scouting or hunting, you learn a little more.

PRUDENCE PAYS

When you enter the woods that first morning of the season, after scouting and learning the general area of a tom, you need to locate his specific area. Don't overuse locator calls. They are certainly of value, but often just standing and listening will tell you where a tom is, and you can move quietly toward him.

Once you have your setup and are settled in with everything in order, don't call until the woods comes alive with other birds and it is light enough for a tom to fly down. And even then, when you make your first call, don't overdo it. If the tom answers, he knows where you are, and calling too much may alert him to your amateur status. I truly believe that unless you are a calling champion, you are better off keeping your calling to a minimum.

I do not believe that anyone can learn to call from reading a book. You have probably already noticed that I use such invented words as "chur chur" and "puck!" for turkey sounds. These are the way turkeys sound to me, and I hope you can identify them from tapes and in the woods. An experienced caller can help you, but in any learning — be it math, a foreign language, first-year anatomy in veterinary college, or how to sing — a person who had a hard time himself makes a better teacher than one to whom the skill came easily. If you have a friend who has the patience to work with you either at home or, better yet, as a hunting team partner, you are in luck.

Of even more value is being able to spend time in the woods just listening. My little tale about the hen that sounded like an unskilled human caller is not exaggerated. After listening to a good tape, hearing the same sound in the woods before the season opens is a thrill. Suddenly there it is, the real thing. Now all you have to do is imitate it with your voice or your artificial call. When you are out of the woods, practice it, and when you suddenly realize that you've gotten it, there is another thrill. You won't be able to wait until the season opens.

Decoys

Until recently the use of decoys in wild turkey hunting was considered a joke by some, by others illegal, and by purists against the rules.

Decoys are now available in all shapes and designs — usually hens, but some are jakes and even toms. Materials used to make them vary from hollow papier-mâché to inflatable plastic, solid molded foam, and foldable foam rubber. Skilled painting with realistic colors makes them appear lifelike. Some are designed to move in the wind, and some have a string attached that you can use to move the head.

USING DECOYS

In a few states and provinces the use of wild turkey decoys is illegal. In most areas the use of decoys that move mechanically is outlawed, as well as those that employ electronic calling. Check your local regulations before using a decoy.

Although I have owned a Carry-Lite brand hollow hen decoy for many years, I have used it very rarely simply because it is just one more awkward thing to carry. But on occasion I have tried it, and felt it helped bring birds in. The new collapsible folding decoys are easier to carry. Under certain conditions — say, at the edge of a meadow surrounded by woods where a tom is apt to hang up on the far side — and if the carrying distance isn't too great, the use of a decoy may be one more thing in your favor.

Archery Equipment

The bows used in deer hunting, if camouflaged, can be used for turkey hunting, but you must consider that when you're turkey hunting you'll be sitting or kneeling, so you will need a shorter bow. A lighter pull should be set for a turkey hunting bow, so that you can stay in a full-draw position for a minute or more. You must wait until the turkey's head is behind a tree to draw, and then hold until the bird moves out to where his small, most vital areas are exposed.

Since you must use both hands to operate the bow, you should be able to call using your voice or a mouth call. If you aren't bothered by its position in your mouth, a diaphragm call might be a good option.

Sighting devices should be kept to a minimum since only the shortest — twenty to twenty-five yards — sighting pins are needed. One bow hunter who is a regular taker of turkeys showed me that his bow is sighted for just twenty yards, eliminating the clutter of too many sighting pins.

Arrows for turkeys should be a dull color or camouflage. Whatever material flies well with your bow is usable, but it should be stiff and light. Carbon-aluminum or graphite shafts are considered most satisfactory.

Most important in bow hunting for turkeys is your choice of broadhead. Because the turkey is a smaller animal, you don't need the penetration that is required for deer hunting. Instead, you want an expand-on-impact broadhead, such as the Punchcutter, with expansion of close to two inches.

Devices to keep the arrow from going clean through the turkey are important too. It is imperative that the arrow stay inside the turkey and cut arteries and veins as he flops. These devices are spiked wire collars referred to as "spiders" or "crickets." They may be found at your archery-supply store.

Other Accessories

You can buy all sorts of accessories, if you wish. A few that might prove useful when you're turkey hunting are blinds, carryalls, and glasses.

Blinds

Blinds are almost a necessity for bow hunters, but are useful for shotgun hunters and photographers as well. Most of the blinds advertised are as heavy as a canvas pup tent and it seems to me that they would be noisy. Some bow hunters have come up with very light net blinds that are easy to transport but keep you invisible from the turkey. (See "Sources," page 162.)

Carryalls

Turkey hunters accumulate more things to carry than are practical for pockets, so I often use something along the lines of a vintage backpack to carry calls, seats, lunch, and thermos as well as my blaze orange vest and hat for coming out of the woods safely.

Several manufacturers have come up with an answer to this problem: turkey hunters' vests. These have all sorts of roomy pockets, a game pocket, a drop-down seat, and two blaze orange patches that may be put on when needed and taken off while on setup. One of these is made by Walls Industries, P.O. Box 98, Cleburne, TX 76031, but there are several others. You may obtain or order them from most sporting-goods stores that cater to turkey hunters.

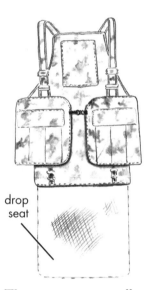

drop seat

There are many carryall vests on the market. This one by Walls has a drop seat and removable blaze orange patches that may be used when a hunter is moving in or out of cover.

Glasses

No matter how good my face covering is, I always feel as though my glasses must look like a pair of headlights to a turkey. There are wrap-around, lightweight camouflage glasses in tinted and clear styles available from CamoVision, P.O. Box 8, Cope, SC 29038 — both clip-on types for those who wear glasses, and regular for those who wear contact lenses or no glasses.

Another solution to the problem of eyeglass reflection is to have an "antireflection" coating applied to your lenses. Your optician can have this done either to new lenses or to those you already have. The main drawback to these is that you must use a special "A-R" lens cleaner; regular lens cleaners may damage the antireflection coating. This is a small price to pay if it will keep your glasses from looking like two mirrors to a turkey.

MISCELLANEOUS EQUIPMENT

- A good knife, sharp and clean to stick and then field dress your bird, should be with you and available.
- You may also want to carry plastic gloves for field dressing and a few paper towels for cleaning up.
- A camouflage seat is useful if you have not bought one of the new vests.
- A blaze orange vest and hat should be part of your equipment for safety reasons. If you hunt in Pennsylvania, you are required by law to wear 250 square inches of blaze orange while walking.
- An often-forgotten item is a camouflage handkerchief to replace the red or white one that might look like a tom's head to an overeager hunter.
- Don't forget string to tie your turkey tag to your prize.

Safety

The rolling, roaring gobble shook the wooded hillside and silenced all the other lesser sounds on this beautiful spring morning. After a moment Jack heard a very soft "chur chur chur," closer to him than the gobble, followed almost immediately by a gobble that reminded him of thunder. His heart pounded with excitement, and he thought, "What good luck. My first day turkey hunting and right over the next rise is a real live hen calling, and beyond her a roaring love-mad tom. All I need to do is sneak up onto the rise; she'll do the calling and, when Mr. Tom shows, I'll have him. All I need to see is his red head, and he's mine."

Ben, another hunter, heard the same gobbles and, despite his years of experience, his heart pounded too. He was set up against a large black oak, perfectly camouflaged, his face blackened by both a two-week growth of beard and makeup. His setup was hidden even further by an upright slab of shale that cast a deep shadow across him and the base of the tree. Ben, however, did not hear the "chur chur chur" as Jack did, because he was the source of it.

A third gobble indicated to Ben that the tom was moving back and forth just out of sight, strutting, waiting for the hen to come to him. Then Ben heard the "whooshaaa whoosh" of the tom inflating and deflating, proving to him that he had surmised correctly about the strutting. He was tempted to call again but decided to leave the call in his mouth and remain quiet.

Jack was making good progress toward the scene, moving a few feet at a time through the damp woods, and using every bit of cover available to hide. He knew that the hunter safety training course he'd taken a few years back had stressed that stalking was dangerous but, to him, this situation — a live hen calling, a tom gobbling beyond — was worth taking a risk.

"What risk?" he thought. "The hen wouldn't be calling and the tom wouldn't be gobbling if another hunter was around. Besides," he thought, "I'm the only one who has permission to hunt these woods since the new owner took over last fall."

Ben was in his glory. He thought, "First day of spring season, at my favorite setup, a tom strutting about eighty yards away. Kind of too bad to fill my tag so easily. Well, if he isn't a good big one I'll just ignore him, but he does sound big. Of course, with the new owner of this property, there might be other hunters coming in and I should take this tom while I have the chance. Should have checked with the new owner, but I've hunted here in this same spot for twenty years. Everyone in the area knows that this is where I hunt."

Another gobble from the tom made the hearts of both Jack and Ben race even faster. Ben decided that perhaps if he called just one more time the tom would quit strutting and come in.

Jack decided to get a little closer. He silently gained a few more yards, just reaching the high point of the rise. He stared ahead toward where the tom was gobbling. He found it difficult to discern objects clearly because of a few large shale ledges and their shadows. He guessed that the hen he had heard call was hidden by one of those shadows. He wished she would call again.

Ben was ready to call, but with his mouth full of saliva he decided he better take the diaphragm call out of his mouth and dry it off. Slowly, quietly, he eased a handkerchief out of his pocket, a tough thing to do with camouflage gloves when you know a tom turkey is eighty yards away. As he eased the handkerchief to his mouth he realized it was his favorite old deer hunting red bandanna, left there since last fall. He thought, "No problem, just have to move more slowly so the tom won't catch the movement."

Jack, now thirty yards away, was trying to make his eyes pierce the shadows and find the hen. He could see movement within the shadows. "It's got to be the hen," he thought, his heart pounding. "Hen? — that's no hen, there's the red head of a tom!"

Jack's 12-gauge roared, and Ben felt as if he had been hit by lightning. Jack rushed toward what he thought was a flopping tom to find a fellow hunter thrashing, with blood coming from his eyes, nose, and mouth. Only a gurgling sound came from Ben. Jack screamed. He threw his gun into the bushes and ran back in the direction he had come from.

The short run back to the road seemed like miles to Jack. He had to get help. A motorist stopped, gathered from the sobbing Jack that a hunter was badly injured in the woods, and punched 911 on his cell phone.

Although in shock, Jack guided rescue squad people to the mercifully unconscious Ben. Then there were sirens screaming, sheriff's questions, and a ride to the local hospital emergency room.

Two hours later Jack, still numb, was told that Ben had died on the operating table.

Jack and Ben are figments of my imagination, and their sad tale was taken from combinations of hunter safety movies I have seen. The shocking thing, however, is that incidents almost identical to this have happened in the past and may happen again, unless every turkey hunter follows safe hunting practices.

As with automobile accidents involving two vehicles, it often takes mistakes by two people to cause hunting accidents. Jack made one serious mistake: He tried to stalk. Despite his experience, Ben made more mistakes, the most serious being the use of the red bandanna handkerchief. Second, Ben had assumed, as too many of us do, that since he'd been hunting in an area for years, every other hunter in the community knew that he was there. Owners change, new hunters come into an area, and cover changes. An orange hat or ribbon on his setup tree might have saved Ben, but after hunting the same spot for years he felt sure there were no other hunters around and, even if there were, they knew he "always hunted that spot."

Of course, Jack and not Ben might have been the man shot had he not been such a quiet stalker, and had Ben been nervous enough to whirl and shoot any sound in the bushes. Jack, too, was wrong in assuming that if an owner told him no one else was hunting on his land, this was fact.

The Most Dangerous Shooting Sport

Statistics show that wild turkey hunting is the most dangerous of the shooting sports. The necessity for full camouflage, the cunning of the quarry, and the excitement of pursuing such a grand trophy are all reasons given for this unwanted distinction. Another factor that makes turkey hunting dangerous is the new magnum loads in all gauges. Wild turkeys are big and tough and difficult to kill, justifying the extra killing power.

However, we must remain constantly aware that although we are carrying shotguns, the range is longer, the shot more penetrating, and another human may be killed or wounded by us at ranges over one hundred yards. Never forget that you have no idea where any other hunter is, or what that hunter is going to do.

You may interpret some of my remarks in this book about "following the rules" of wild turkey hunting as somewhat overcritical. This is not my intent. Whether it be wild turkey hunting, golf, fox hunting, tennis, or thoroughbred racing, a sport has to have rules. I do sincerely believe if all turkey hunters hunted by the rules, turkey hunting accidents would be almost unheard of.

Don'ts and Dos

A few of the most common mistakes are:

- Stalking
- Shooting at anything other than a turkey's head and neck
- Trying to "drive" turkeys, as is done with deer
- Not knowing where other hunters are, what is beyond your target, and what is between you and your target
- Wearing red, white, or blue
- Using a "gobble" call

Those are the most common "don'ts." Here are a few "dos":

- Wear a blaze orange hat or vest when you're going in to hunt or coming out carrying a turkey.
- If there is time, put a blaze orange hat above you at your setup. A blaze orange ribbon of surveyor's tape is useful too, but don't leave a loose end to blow in the breeze — movement may scare turkeys.
- When field dressing your turkey, wear a blaze orange vest. A hat alone won't be seen by a hunter coming up behind you.
- Before you run to a turkey you have shot, put the safety on your gun.
- With all the things a turkey hunter carries, a tiny cellular telephone is a good addition for safety, and invaluable if you get hurt or have a problem. Let's hope you never need it except to call home and say, "Get the camera ready, I'm coming home with a big one."

In addition, note the sidebar "Safety Tips" in other chapters.

If you make a mistake or see another hunter make a mistake that could have resulted in an accident, don't be ashamed to tell other hunters. Airplane pilots tell each other of their mistakes and how they corrected them, in the hope that this may help save someone else. Turkey hunting is a comparatively new sport. We all need to help each other make it safer.

TURKEY HUNTING ETIQUETTE

- Secure the landowner's permission and learn the boundaries by scouting before you hunt.
- Try to find out who else might be hunting in the area and try to meet them, or at least talk by phone, so you do not overlap.
- When you do meet another hunter in the woods, make your presence known by speaking audibly and, if necessary, by waving an orange hat — not by using a turkey call or shouting.
- If the other hunter is set up, after making sure he or she knows of your presence, turn and leave.
- If you are sure the other hunter is not supposed to be there, go speak to him or her and try to settle the matter without loud talk. You may find out you are in the wrong; you may be able to work out a plan that will not spoil the day's hunting for both of you.
- When you receive a landowner's permission, it should be clear to both of you whether the permission is for you alone or if you may bring another hunter. For landowners, this is a particularly sore spot. All too often the person given permission doesn't mention that he or she hunts with one or more other people.
- If the landowner is not a hunter, the gift from you of a nicely cleaned, picked bird may guarantee you a place to hunt for years to come.

Spring Hunt

Soft, damp darkness enveloped us as we left the warmth and light of the car and started up the abandoned dirt road that had been, on its most glorious day in December 1775, the path of General Henry Knox. He, his men, and his oxen used this trail to travel with the cannon they were transporting from Ticonderoga to Boston. This day, too, was a historic day for Bill and me and a few hundred other aspiring wild turkey hunters. It was the first New York wild turkey season ever. The wild turkey had at one point become practically extinct in New York state.

We were experienced deer and duck hunters, having learned since boyhood from experience and from other hunters. We had observed wild turkeys in the fields and seen them in the woods during deer season since their reintroduction into eastern New York. However, what we knew about hunting them was worse than nothing, since what we had been told and read was mostly all wrong.

Our only advantages were the experience of hunting together and having scouted the area ahead of us, where we knew there were wild turkeys. This could not make up for the store of misinformation that led us, along with most other local would-be turkey hunters, to stop along roads in the area for weeks before the season and practice calling, to see if we'd hear a gobble in reply.

Our plan seemed good enough. We were going to hike up the trail to the top of the wooded ridge, wait until we heard a gobble, and then set up, with the shooter between the tom and the caller. Knowing that the law permitted bearded toms only, I had looked at a silhouette of a wild turkey the night before just to ascertain exactly what part of his anatomy the beard hung from.

We walked in silence and reached the top of the ridge long before the first hint of light. Working to the left of the trail to a higher spot, we stood listening. Seconds later we heard a gobble, then another and another, from all directions. We were bewildered: The gobbles seemed to us to be too artificial. Yes, we were surrounded, but were we surrounded by turkeys or by other hunters using gobble calls and answering each other?

As Bill scraped leaves, looking for bare ground to stand on more quietly, he found what felt to his foot like a hard, flat stone surface. He scraped more away with his hand, then looked with a flashlight and saw that he was standing on a gravestone.

The first thing he could decipher was a burial date of May 1878, and then an 1850 birth date, of a young woman. This had been a cleared farm area a century earlier, and we were standing on what had probably been a family burial ground. Clearing more leaves revealed more stones, and a sobering story. Here on this hilltop, among a few other stones, were the graves of an entire young family — mother, father, and three young children — all of whom died in May 1878.

We stood in silence, awed by our find, forgetting the original purpose of our journey. Suddenly the ratchetlike call and "rat tat tat" of a woodpecker jarred us from our thoughts of the difficult and fragile life of the people who worked this hill farm a century before. This was followed by another call in the opposite direction.

The first blue-gray light of dawn was showing to the east. The almost silent woods came alive with bird calls that we were not at all familiar with, as well as the fluttering sounds of small wings that we were used to hearing in the alders surrounding a duck blind in October.

The gobbles continued as we moved in the direction of the closest one, still wondering if it was real or another hunter. Considering safety, we abandoned our original plan and separated, each of us finding a tree stout enough to set up by, out of range of each other.

I wish I could say that beginner's luck prevailed and that after my first try with my box call there came an answer, followed by the flapping of a fly down. Nothing of the sort happened. The gobbles continued, I heard fly downs, but none came closer. Far off on another ridge I heard one lone shot, but nothing close up. At seven o'clock, as agreed, we started out of the woods to head to work.

Back at the car we vowed two things. One was to return to that burial plot, write down the names from the stones, and, if we couldn't find descendants, try to restore the site. Second, we agreed to learn more about wild turkeys and wild turkey hunting before we went into the woods on a spring hunt again. The first vow was never accomplished, but the second, twenty years later, is still in progress.

Before you start to hunt wild turkeys, you need to learn all you can by reading, listening to other hunters, attending turkey hunting seminars, and observing wild turkeys. On your first hunt and every hunt thereafter you will learn more, develop new techniques, and realize that some of what is good technique for one hunter may not work at all for you.

Scouting

Scouting territory is probably the most important, and most neglected, part of turkey hunting. Unless you want and can afford to use a guide, you have to scout.

Hopefully, you have a general idea of where you would like to hunt. Riding the roads looking for wild turkeys in this area during early morning and late afternoon is a start. Just because you see a flock of turkeys feeding in a field in January doesn't mean they will be there during spring season, but they will often stay within the general area.

Whatever you do, don't use a turkey call from the road when scouting, as many of us, in our ignorance, did years ago. A tom can only be fooled by a particular call once. Owl, crow, and even bull elk calls and car door slams will elicit a gobble from a roosting tom without spoiling the hunting for you and every other hunter.

Having breakfast at the local diner and listening to the conversations there may give you "intelligence" as to where turkeys are being seen. School bus drivers, R.F.D. mail carriers, and United Parcel Service drivers are all good people to get to know. These folks are riding the roads day after day and can't help but notice wildlife.

Get to know landowners in the area. If you can strike up a friendship, they are apt to tell you where they are seeing birds. You may find that it is easier to secure permission to hunt wild turkeys on private property than to hunt deer. Turkey hunters have so far not had their reputation spoiled, as deer hunters have, by a thoughtless few. The short range of the shotgun does not conjure up the same fear in people's minds that the long range of the deer rifle does. Still, it is the *hunter* who creates the image of danger to others. It is up to all of us to keep our good reputation.

Try to find out if other turkey hunters are expecting to hunt in the area you have selected. If at all possible, get to know these people so you each have an idea where the others will be. Ethics dictate that if you happen upon another hunter already set up, you withdraw. If hunters have been using a particular spot for many seasons, they may feel they have "grandfather rights." Even if you own

Male turkeys are said to leave "J" shaped droppings, and females round piles.

the land you are hunting on, a confrontation can be avoided by proper planning and communication prior to opening day.

Once you have turkeys located in a general area and have permission to hunt, do some walking to really get to know the territory. This can be done anytime to learn the contour and general characteristics of the land. You should be looking for likely trees, or areas of trees, whose diameter is sufficient to hide the width of your body. Look for places that have easy access so you can find your way into the area in the dark, places to hide your vehicle from the turkeys' roosting area, and alternate routes in and out. Keep an eye on the ground for tracks, feathers, feeding scratches, and droppings. Droppings can indicate the sex of turkeys: a J shape for a male, round or piled up for a female.

Try to learn the differences between feeding signs of white-tailed deer, squirrels, and turkeys. A scratching turkey tends to throw leaves in all directions; deer and squirrels, in one or two directions, front and back. Deer feeding on beechnuts will sometimes leave long, two-sided furrows through loose, dry leaves. Do not confuse feeding signs with buck deer scrapings,

Feeding turkeys scatter leaves in all directions, but more in the direction opposite the direction the flock is moving.

Look for telltale three toed scratches in the earth, and for an occasional feather.

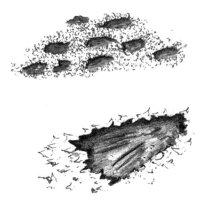

When a deer feeds, he pushes leaves aside with his nose instead of scratching indiscriminately, as does a turkey.

Squirrels are more apt than deer or turkeys to dig small holes where they feed. Squirrels also leave nut shells or other food particles.

where you may see leaves thrown in all directions but that go down to bare earth, with generally a hoofprint or two in the dirt.

Starting about a week before the season opens, listen near your proposed hunting site just prior to first light and just before dusk. Some people recommend using owl calls to trick roosting toms into gobbling. I prefer to just listen, or to use my owl hoot sparingly. Then see if there is a pattern to the sounds, such as a dominant deep-toned gobble that always comes from a certain hillside. If so, and if you "put the tom to bed" the night before hunting and have picked out a good tree to set up by, your chances of finding him there the next morning are good. That is, if a dozen or so of the gremlins that protect big tom turkeys don't interfere.

Fresh only in the fall rutting season, deer "scrapes" can be confused with turkey feeding signs. To distinguish between the two, look for a buck's hoofprint and a broken or chewed limb overhead.

If you did your scouting more than a week before the first day of the season, particularly if there is a sudden change in weather, such as a late-spring snow, repeat, looking for fresh tracks, feeding evidence, and droppings.

Classic Spring Hunt

Every wild turkey hunter has a fantasy about the perfect hunt. Sooner or later it will happen, if you don't give up. It goes sort of like this:

During the fall hunt there is a flock of fourteen mature toms hanging by themselves. You see them at a distance — close enough to know that at least one has a beard literally dragging on the ground — but never close enough for a shot. They appear when you least expect them, and just as quickly disappear like a mirage.

During deer season other hunters see the same flock and always talk about the big old beard dragger. "Hope he winters well, because come spring I'm going to have him!" more than one hunter exclaims.

Winter comes early, cold with deep snow, great for cross-country skiing but rough on turkeys. While skiing, you see the turkeys still in flocks of twenty to thirty, sometimes sitting in the trees over the ski trail, apparently eating birch and poplar buds. You also see them following a manure spreader, picking the chunks of corn left undigested by the cows.

A January thaw gives the birds a break. For a few days there is even bare ground and they can feed on cornfield waste, wild cherry pits, sumac, and acorns found under the leaves on the oak-forested hillside.

In late February winter returns with a vengeance. Snow is so deep that the farmers in the valley don't even try to spread manure, but pile it until spring. A flock of ninety hens and young birds is seen near the biggest dairy, feeding at the trench silo and around the feed racks. You also see them in the streambed and along its bank, where buds from alders and willows are apparently available.

The farmer tells you that besides the big flock, there is now a second flock of twenty-eight, all mature toms and two-year-old jakes. When they come, the hens and young birds leave. He says there is at least one big beard dragger and several more with beards touching the snow as they walk.

One day while you're getting ready to leave the road on skis, you see across the way that the field below the dairy barn, where the stream cuts through, is black with turkeys. The snow apparently has blown away and they are trying to find food in the bare patches, and scratching to reach remnants of cornfield waste. The farmer says he believes they have lost all fear.

Suddenly the flock disperses, flying in all directions, landing in small trees and running in small groups across the field. Directly over them is a small helicopter, perhaps five hundred feet in the air. You realize the turkeys have not lost all fear; they must think the copter is a huge great horned owl, their mortal enemy.

Spring comes suddenly in late March. The big flock breaks up into smaller ones, and it is possible from the highway to see toms blown all out of proportion, strutting, showing off in front of the hens. After this rough winter, where do they get their energy? Every one looks as big as the monster beard dragger. But your fantasy must be realized: You have to locate him, call him in, and for once get yourself a bragging-size turkey.

You scout the area, listening each dawn and dusk for a week before opening day. There are lots of gobbles but, perhaps by wishful thinking, you feel you have located the big one's roosting area. The evening before the season opens you hear his deep gobble on the hillside, warning all that every hen within sound of his call is his, and any jake or young tom that gets in his way will be cut to pieces by his spurs. That night you don't sleep a wink.

The next morning you hike up the jeep trail through the black birches that now cover the pasture of years gone by. Through the gap in the stone wall that runs parallel to the hill, you come to a clearing between the hemlocks to the north and the oaks to the south, where you're sure the old tom beard dragger is roosting.

There are several ancient wild apple trees in the clearing, along with a few thorn apple bushes and black birches. One apple tree is big enough to cover your back. You long ago cleared the area around it of leaves, twigs, and stones too hard to sit on. Behind you are some dense hemlock woods, a favorite roosting place for hens not already nesting. Ahead of you, fifty yards away, is another stone wall running up and down the hill, with a twenty-foot gap in it cleared by loggers many years ago. Beyond the gap is a hillside of fifty acres of mostly oaks, but with hickories, hard maples, ashes, a few poplars, and even a few American chestnuts trying to survive.

You settle down on your camouflage seat with your back to the apple-tree trunk. You put your kit bag where you can reach it, your slate call in your lap, and your other two box calls within reach. Your loaded shotgun is across your right leg so you are ready for the old tom when he comes through the gap. You have on your oldest faded camouflage coveralls, camouflage cotton gloves, and camouflage face net over your hat. You relax and listen.

You hear the milking machine vacuum pump sputter, half a mile to the north, smooth out, and start to run. Far to the south you hear a rooster's crow and, almost as it fades, a gobble far off in that same direction. Then up the valley comes the sound of a diesel. As it reaches the frost bump near the foot of the hill the fifth wheel gives a "kerbump!" sound like a far-off artillery piece. There is no time for an echo — the truck sound is followed immediately by a great roaring, rolling gobble. To this there is an echo far up the peak behind you. You feel the hair on the back of your neck stand up.

All is silent for a few minutes, but for the pounding of your heart. Then ever so softly behind you, you hear "chur chur chur." Behind you again you hear wing and feather noises. Then ahead of you, another roaring gobble, followed by a second. The noise in the tree behind you continues, and as the first real light filters down you hear "flap flap flapflaplaplaplap — thud." The hen is down, and you hope she'll call or old Mister Big will fly down and come over to investigate. Still, up here under the shoulder of the peak, it is too dark to see well enough to shoot.

Ten minutes that seem like an hour go by, with Mister Big roaring out about once a minute, and other gobbles much farther away. There is no other sound from the hen, and you hope that, wishing no contact with an amorous tom today, she has left the area.

As it becomes lighter you make up your mind that it is now or never. You give a very tiny "scree scree scree" on your slate, which is answered with a roaring gobble. It is such a temptation to call again, but time is on your side and you don't want to appear too eager. You'll make him come to you. One more gobble, then silence, followed by stirring sounds you hope come from his tree.

Then it happens: "flap flap flapflaplaplaplap — thud." You hear rustling, and the "whooshaaa whoosh" that should mean he is puffing himself up. Through the gap in the stone wall you can make him out, strutting in the early-morning gloom. Then up goes his head, and a roaring gobble sounds. You are afraid to try the slate because your hand will shake and spoil the call. You are afraid to move, to even blink or breathe.

Now the tom goes out of sight behind the wall to the left of the gap, and you are sure you have lost him. In desperation you try the little plunger box — less chance to make a mistake than with the slate and shaking hands. Again he roars and comes through the gap in the wall, only to blow himself up again and go into a strut.

This time he is in range but you must wait for him to have his head behind a tree. He moves very slowly, and it seems like forever, but after a bit his head goes behind a tree. Up comes your shotgun, the crosshairs are just past the tree, and as the red head appears you hold it a bit high and squeeze it off. A great flopping of wings, and all is quiet. With the safety on your gun, you run as fast as you can toward where you last saw him.

Then . . . there he is, lying on his side, without a quiver, his great red head around on his breast, with that long, long beard. You stand with your gun at the ready, staring at him, feeling a little sad, and wondering if you should offer a prayer from your heart to the Great Spirit, as the Native Americans were said to have done. You take it all in, and hope you can keep the memory of this morning forever.

To most people, and rightly so, the classic spring hunt, calling a tom into shotgun range, is the greatest challenge. To some it is just *turkey hunting* — that is it, nothing else counts.

Besides the game law regulations governing wild turkey hunting, there are many rules that turkey hunters impose upon themselves. As with the rules of golf or fox hunting, transgressions are known only to the participant and punished only by his or her conscience. Conversely, the pride and joy you receive from bagging a spring tom are in proportion to how well you observed the rules.

Meeting the Challenge

After you have located a tom by hearing his gobble, whether he is still in his tree in the early morning or on a distant ridge at 10 A.M., just getting close enough without alerting him is your first challenge. The proper location of your setup is more important than the distance: If you have heard him, he can certainly hear not only your call but also the noise you create by moving in the woods.

Knowing your territory — easily followed deer trails, woods roads, and open places that may be quietly traversed — gives you an advantage. You should also be aware of obstructions, such as stone walls, fences, ledges, streams, and heavy brush, that will cause a tom to "hang up." There may come a time and circumstance when you will move away from the tom, circle, and reapproach him from a different direction.

Setting Up

Move as quietly as possible until you come to a tree, preferably large enough to shield your body from behind and your outline from the direction you expect the tom to come from.

The ideal setup tree should have no hanging branches or small saplings around it that would prevent a full 270-degree swing of your gun barrel. Preferably, you will have time to clear away leaves, dead sticks, and stones if they prevent you from sitting quietly and comfortably. There is a trade-off between the noise you make doing this and the advantage of being comfortable and quiet. I like to have a few potential setup trees picked out and cleared around in advance, although things seldom work out just right for me to use them. If they did, I would not have the same challenge.

Some early turkey hunting books said that the hunter should be on higher ground than the tom; that he comes uphill more easily. My experience is just the reverse, that toms come downhill. It is important that you have relatively level ground for at least fifty yards in front of you. A rise in

Ideal setup locations shield the hunter from behind, have no blind spots in front where a bird may suddenly appear, and have no brush or overhanging branches that can interfere with lateral movement of his gun. This hunter is alert and at the ready, his gun already up, supported by his knees, so he does not need to raise it when a bird appears.

front of you gives the tom a chance to sneak up on you so that when you finally see him, he is so close that he sees your eyes blink.

Sometimes a tom, and very often a jake, will come in from behind you. If your tree is wide enough he will at least be off to your side before he is able to see you.

Once you are settled on your camouflage pad, your face mask and camouflage gloves on, with your loaded shotgun across your legs in the direction you expect the bird to come from, sit quietly and listen. Don't be in a hurry to call, since the tom you heard may have heard your movements too. Unless you hear the unmistakable sound of a fly down or a good strong gobble, wait at least five minutes, and if it is still too dark to see well on the ground, wait longer.

Calling and Listening

When you do call, in early morning try a really soft tree call, sort of a little "chur chur chur." In midmorning you can use a more vigorous yelp, but you should still play the part of a rather bashful young hen. If you get an answer, don't reply at once — play hard to get.

If you hear a hen near you making a tree call, don't do anything. She may fly down and call herself, or she may fly down and take off away from the tom. If so, give her time to leave, and then try a yelp call. Some experienced hunters imitate the sound of a fly down by slapping a thigh, and even imitate the landing thud with their fist on the ground. Then they stir up a few leaves to imitate the sound of a feeding hen scratching. Until you feel confident that you can do all these things without making a mistake, it is best to keep it simple. Unlike duck hunting, less calling is better.

Just because you don't hear a gobble, don't assume there is no tom on his way in. On mornings when a front or storm is coming in, no matter how clear and bright, the turkeys will be quiet. If such is the case, and you are sure there are turkeys in the vicinity, sit, listen, and watch. Every few minutes give a series of soft calls, and then wait again.

There are sounds besides gobbles you should be listening for on these quiet days. One is the soft, airy "whooshaaa whoosh" sound of the gobbler inflating himself as he struts. Another is the sound a jake makes, sort of a high-pitched "churrp." Of course, you may also hear turkeys rustling the leaves as they walk. If you hear any of these, freeze, and don't move until you make out where and what the sound is.

One sound you don't want to hear is the "puck! puck!" alarm that a hen makes when she discovers you and wants to warn every other turkey for half a mile around. Another sound that will spoil your morning is the loud "woosh woosh woosh" of a white-tailed doe that has winded you and is warning every creature for acres around.

When you are being answered, play it coy, and don't make your calls too urgent. Remember, the tom expects the hen to come to him.

> **SAFETY TIP**
>
> Never try to stalk a gobbler! It could be another hunter. Another hunter may also be waiting for the gobbler you are stalking, and shoot.

Patience Pays Off

If a gobbler does hang up, going back and forth at right angles to your line of sight, be patient. Try a different call and wait; he may eventually give in and come in. Or you may try going away from him, calling, and then going partway back. He may think the hen has left and follow her, coming directly at you. If this doesn't work and you are certain there are no other hunters in the area, work back and around to one end or the other of his strut area.

When a gobbler does come within range, he doesn't usually come in a direct line, straight at you. More than likely he'll come at an angle, or even try to circle you. Don't move anything but your eyeballs until his head is behind a tree. This is the most critical time of the whole hunt. Release your safety, raise your gun, and aim a little high, just past the tree where you expect his head to reappear. When the red head appears, squeeze off.

A second shot is seldom needed or even possible. Most birds will go into a flopping motion or even rise up into the air a bit, then come down. Some will drop and lie perfectly still. Put the safety on your gun and run to where you last saw him. Be ready to shoot again if his head is up and he starts running or flying; flopping birds with their heads down are already dead. Hopefully, you have put one or more pellets in his head and several more in his neck. If so, he is your bird. Congratulations!

Using Decoys

A young friend of mine started hunting wild turkey only a few years ago as a means of relaxation from his demanding job as an electronics specialist on an Air Force C-130 ski-equipped cargo plane. He leads what many of us would think of as an adventurous, exciting life — flying to such places as McMurdo Sound and the South Pole. Still, after one of these trips he is ready for a change of pace.

Learning about wild turkeys is just as fascinating, yet relaxing, to him as the intricate communications equipment he works with. His attention to detail and ability to learn earned him a fine turkey the first time he went fall hunting. His next goal was to become a successful spring hunter in the classic sense, calling in and shooting a trophy tom.

He has become a skilled caller, taken some good birds, but still hadn't taken a really "big one" until recently. Then his wife presented him with a wild turkey decoy, and although it seemed to him just one more thing to carry into the woods, he agreed to take it the first day he had off during the spring season.

Working along the edge of a field at the foot of a wooded hillside, he reached his destination just after first light. Across a stone wall that intersected this long narrow field, and through a small copse of trees two hundred yards away, he spotted two black dots that appeared to be turkeys. He crossed the wall, found a tree for a setup, and settled down. As the sky became lighter, he gave a call.

The two birds — by now he was sure they were a pair of hens — looked toward him, then continued to feed. In the woods beyond them he heard a gobble. Crawling through the trees toward the edge of the field, he placed the decoy in the open and crawled back to his setup.

Again he called. This time the "hens" looked toward him and, much to his surprise, extended their necks and ran directly toward the decoy. At the same time a large bird came into view and then began to skirt the meadow through the trees toward him.

As the first two birds closed in my friend ascertained that they were jakes — but the bird coming through the trees was a very large tom. When the jakes reached the decoy they stopped and looked toward the oncoming tom. The tom seemed intent on charging the jakes, giving my friend the opportunity to raise his gun and shoot.

On the scales the tom weighted twenty-three pounds, making the weight of the decoy insignificant on the way back to the vehicle.

To my young electronics friend, decoys are a valuable hunting aid. I don't expect to see him in the woods without one.

One situation in spring hunting in which a decoy is indicated is when bringing in call-shy toms — birds that have been fooled by calling but not shot, and are still looking for hens but won't come to an artificial call. If you can put such a tom to bed (that is, hear him call as he goes to roost), try putting a decoy within sight of his tree in the very early morning darkness, but don't attempt to call. At daylight he may see the decoy and fly down to it.

Here's another use of the hen decoy for the call-shy tom: Place your decoy in a spot that you know he frequents, and either wait or call just once to get his attention.

The position of the decoy is the most important factor in its successful, safe use. Position your decoy in the open, twenty to thirty yards from your setup, not directly in front of you but at an angle on the side you are more comfortable shooting at.

Hunters who regularly use decoys with success all say that calling should be kept to a minimum. Once you call, the tom knows exactly where you are; if you continue he'll realize that the call and the decoy are in two different locations, alerting him to danger. A tom coming in to a decoy is intent on the decoy and less apt to see the hunter raise the shotgun. This perhaps is the greatest advantage in using decoys.

SAFETY TIP

When positioning your decoy, you should also take into consideration the danger of another hunter shooting at it. This is particularly true if you are using jake or tom decoys, or in fall when either sex may be taken.

To the purist who believes that the only proper way to hunt wild turkeys is in spring with no aid but a call, the use of decoys is cheating. I admire these individuals the way I do the people who climb Mount Everest or run the Boston Marathon. Still, if a hunter has met his match, a tom he just can't call in, and outsmarts him with a decoy, that hunter deserves some admiration too.

Team Hunting

An avid turkey hunter I often think of was one of five brothers. As boys they all developed a love of hunting; ring-necked pheasants were their main game but rabbits, squirrels, and once in a while a grouse or woodcock were bonuses. They hunted as a team in their youth, the older brothers helping the younger.

As they passed from boyhood to young adulthood they still hunted together as much as the mature responsibilities of job and family would permit. As white-tailed deer became more plentiful, they found that teamwork was a real help in bringing down a buck.

Then suddenly, and something they never dreamed of as boys, wild turkeys became available. Completely new hunting techniques and skills had to be developed. They found that turkey hunting, unlike all the other hunting they had done, was a lonely sport — just the individual hunter against the wily tom turkey, with all the "rules" favoring the tom. The area around their deer camp became prime turkey habitat, but although all five brothers spent time turkey hunting, only Frank, the middle brother, regularly tagged a bird.

The brother who was a horseman, my client and friend, compared it with fishing: "When we were kids we'd all go fishing, same tackle, same lures, and same spot. Frank would catch fish and the rest of us would go home with empty baskets."

But instead of blaming it all on luck, the brothers decided that Frank was the better caller, and that once Frank got his bird he was going to have to call for them.

In our state, once you filled your tag you could no longer hunt, but if unarmed you could call for another hunter. The five brothers observed the law; working as a two-person team, with Frank calling and one of the others positioned ahead of him, well camouflaged, they brought in their full share of toms. For them turkey hunting became another team sport.

Even to the purist, who considers any variation from the classic spring hunt — locating a tom, calling him in, and shooting him with no help from any other person or device — against the rules, some variations in hunting technique are tolerated.

In most sports, allowances are made to make contests more even, such as using less weight on the horse that is a nonwinner or has an apprentice jockey, or the handicaps in golf. Considering that the ability to call varies from person to person, like the ability to sing or play a musical instrument, allowing team hunting doesn't seem unfair.

To team hunt, a gobbler must be located, or at least his location must be surmised, before the positioning of the caller and the hunter. The technique of team hunting varies mostly in the positioning of the team. The caller should be positioned on the far side of the shooter, away from where the tom is expected to come in. When turkeys come in on a straight line, things usually end in the shooter's favor. However, the tom often sneaks in from behind.

Safety considerations should be foremost. As long as the caller carries no gun, there is no danger that he or she will shoot the team partner. The shooter has a better chance if he or she is thirty yards or so from the caller, since the tom will be concentrating on where the call came from. But if too far away, there is a danger that the turkey will get between the caller and the shooter.

To avoid this, the two partners may be on opposite sides of a large tree. Next best is for the caller's setup to be against a second large tree behind and at an angle of fifteen to thirty degrees to the right of a right-handed shooter, or the left of a left-handed shooter.

Thorough scouting may find such trees for possible setups for team hunting. However, in the real world, with a gobbler sounding off in the dark, the team must improvise and make the best of what they find at hand to quickly and quietly set up. A good team must be able to work together and understand each other without talking.

The use of a decoy in team hunting certainly improves the chance of a bird being taken. Net blinds, for the caller and even the shooter, are called for too, particularly if the shooter is wielding a bow instead of a shotgun.

When Toms Don't Gobble

Almost everything written about hunting the wild turkey in spring involves hearing the gobble of a tom. Listen to a discussion among wild turkey hunters and the main topic talked about is hunting when the toms *don't* gobble. A common admonishment from an experienced hunter to a discouraged novice is, "Just because you don't hear a gobble doesn't mean there are no turkeys."

Earlier in this book I mentioned that even on a beautiful spring morning, if a storm is in the offing or a cold front is moving in, toms may be silent. Some hunters believe that the weather is only part of the answer, however; they'll tell you that as each year of turkey hunting goes by, the toms that are noisy are killed off and the smart silent ones are left to pass on their genes.

Whether it is the weather or the gene pool or both, you must be ready to change technique, be more diligent, and be far more focused to bag a silent tom. In addition, selection of a site for your setup must take into consideration that the silent tom does not give any warning. Suddenly, he is there. Chances are that he was peeking at and studying you through the underbrush long before you saw him. Only if you sit stone still and quiet will he come close enough for you to see him.

The general location of the silent tom may be found by scouting — you might see turkeys move from a feeding area into the woods at roosting time, for instance. However, the exact location of your setup may depend on your own intuition.

The site of your setup for hunting silent toms is most important. There should be no underbrush curtain close by in any direction from which a tom could invisibly spy on you. The ground should be reasonably level or on an even slope. You don't want the tom popping up over a rise of ground five yards away.

Once you have decided on the possible location of a tom, select a setup, settle down, and, after a reasonable time for all to become quiet, call softly, just one series. Don't give up too quickly. If nothing appears, call softly again after about fifteen minutes. Again, don't be discouraged if you have to wait an hour. Enjoy the other sounds of the woods. Every fifteen minutes or so, call softly.

After an hour or so, use your intuition. You may want to move to another location, some distance away. Remember that a turkey's hearing is almost like radar. If he was anywhere near, he has heard you and decided you aren't a hen. Hope that in another location another tom may hear your call and come in.

Any tom, particularly a silent one, is liable to come in from where you don't expect him, such as right up the trail you walked in on not fifteen minutes before. For this reason the tree for your setup must be wide enough to hide you so that the tom must come around to your side-vision area to see you. If you hear any noise, such as rustling leaves behind you, don't look around the tree. Freeze and hope it is a turkey, and that he'll come into view so you at least have a chance, slim as it might be.

When you suddenly do see him, any reaction on your part will send him off. You must be immobile and hope that he will move to get a better look at you and, in doing so, leave his head behind a tree long enough for you to raise your gun, release the safety, and, as his head reappears, shoot.

Silent toms are the most difficult to bag, but if you do bring one down, you can take pride in your superior hunting skills.

Other Spring Hunt Variations

The spring hunt can have many variations. Here's a brief look at a few of the more common ones. Choose one that suits your preferences or the conditions of your particular hunting site.

The Late-Morning Hunt

The classic spring hunt seems to involve arising hours before sunrise. I find more and more hunters scorning this early hour and waiting until midmorning, when the toms have bred the available hens, had a little to eat, and are on the prowl for more hens. This seems to work best late in the season, when there aren't that many hens waiting to be bred.

For someone of my nature who enjoys walking in the woods, this late-morning hunting is a pleasure. Other hunters have gone to breakfast or to work, and I have the woods to myself. If I hear a gobble, fine. I get as close as I can, set up, and call. Or, more likely, I won't hear any gobbles but will set up in a pleasant place, call a bit, and just wait.

At these times, if a bird comes in it is often on the quiet; he sees me before I see him. If I freeze until he starts to circle and gets his head behind a tree, I've got my bird; if not, he and I have both had an adventure.

When Toms Roost with Hens

Another variation in technique is used when toms roost with a flock of hens. You are there in the morning, call, hear the tom gobble and later come down, but off tom goes with his harem, scorning the best call you put out. Some hunters facing such a situation go to the roosting area just at dusk the evening before and scare the flock, scattering them. The next morning, hopefully, the tom will gobble and the hunter will be there to answer, getting a chance for a shot when tom comes to the artificial call.

Whether the above is considered within the rules of turkey hunting etiquette, or for that matter even legal, I cannot say. I certainly recommend researching the game laws in your own area before trying it. As to the morals of it, I believe it's up to your own conscience. The more frustrated and desperate you become after being spurned by "a tom in the trees with hens," the less censorious your conscience will be.

Tree Stands

One of the largest turkeys I ever saw was shot from a tree stand. Most true spring turkey hunters consider this blasphemy, but at least two hunters I know use tree stands when available. One calls from ground level but stops calling and scurries up the far side of the tree when the tom answers. The other hunter uses a tree stand without even calling. In his words, "I just wait until a turkey comes along." I am not advocating either of these methods, but mention them only as variations of the classic technique.

Bow Hunting

There is a man who bow hunts wild turkeys both spring and fall in the same area where I hunt. He uses a decoy and shoots from a net blind. His success rate is better than mine with my Ithaca Mag 10.

Besides good equipment and almost continual practice with the bow to be accurate, he has other things going for him. One is patience, another is persistence, and a third is profound understanding and respect for nature. He hunts nearly every day of the season until he fills his tags. Late in the season, when everyone else has given up, he is still out there.

The bow hunter must have a thorough understanding of the anatomy of the turkey. Despite the turkey's size, the area where he may be hit and brought down by hitting his spine with an arrow is very small. Hits in other places, such as the heart-and-lung area, are likely to be fatal but will not paralyze the bird, and he will go a long way before dying.

For a shot at a turkey coming straight at you, aim just above the beard. From the side, aim at the butt of the wing. From the rear, shoot for the base of the tail, which can be accomplished only when the tom is in strut with the tail spread.

A plus for bow hunting is that few landowners will refuse a lone bow hunter permission to be on their land.

As mentioned in chapter 5, which includes information on archery equipment for hunting wild turkeys, you must be able to mouth-call when bow hunting, since you need both hands to handle a bow.

Next to trying a "kill or miss" shot at the turkey's head, a shot from the side at the butt of the wing is best.

From the front, an arrow hitting just above the beard will do the job. A bit off and the arrow may wound and not put the bird down.

Least desirable is a shot from the rear while the bird is fanned. If the arrow hits the spine, he will go down; if not he may run off, but die later.

For you who may find shotgun hunting a bit old hat and want to be challenged a bit more, get the equipment, take some lessons, practice, and give bow hunting a try.

Fall Hunt

The stock of Joe's 20-gauge seemed to move imperceptibly from sight. The only sound was the moaning of the wind in the white pines to my right. Behind me and to my left was the base of a giant old butternut. Beyond the tree, leaning against the other side, was my twelve-year-old grandson Joe. Beyond Joe was a stone wall, and beyond the wall a well-gleaned cornfield. Along the wall and through the remains of the barbed-wire fence stood now leafless chokecherry trees. It was 11 A.M. on a windy, raw November morning and we had been sitting like this since 7. Until a minute before, three inches of the stock of Joe's Mag 20-gauge youth pump had been visible to me out of the corner of my left eye.

We knew turkeys had been feeding along this wall, probably on the seeds from the chokecherries. There certainly wasn't any corn left. This was the third and last day of a three-day first hunting experience for Joe. He had gotten a gray squirrel, missed a grouse, and the evening before, although surrounded by turkeys, hadn't been able to get off a shot before they spotted him and flew. No amount of calling succeeded in bringing them back. I waited now, still as could be, to hear him shoot, but all I could hear was the wind in the pines.

During these three days the usually talkative Joe had been quiet. I would have suspected he was sad or homesick had I not seen him this way on an afternoon before he was to pitch at a ball game. Joe was "focusing," as his baseball coach had taught him. This time, though, he was focusing on hunting turkeys, on gun safety, and on all the things he'd learned in the twelve-hour hunter safety training course he'd taken the previous August.

I wondered if, like the evening before, he had perhaps gotten a touch of "buck fever" and, if there were turkeys out there, was just waiting too long to shoot. I could feel myself shivering, and hoped if there were turkeys they wouldn't hear me. A friend told me once that no matter how excited you get with a son or daughter's first deer, squirrel, or whatever, when a grandchild has a success it really gets to you.

All this was going through my mind for what seemed like forever, but probably wasn't more than a minute. I wonder now who had the "buck fever," Joe or Grandpa. When the little 20-gauge finally roared, it was a relief, but then other doubts came into my mind. Although it had patterned well, was the 20 enough gun for the size turkey Joe was waiting for, and did he remember to aim high at the head?

"Got him, Grandpa."

What a relief! And even more so when I looked around the butternut into the field to see the bright red head lying limp over the side of a very large, very dead turkey.

Guns were unloaded, the tag filled out, and then we headed home for pictures. Joe took part in the plucking and asked for only a little guidance as he dressed his own bird. With the cooling carcass of the big turkey in a tub of ice water, Joe became his talkative self again. You can't stay focused all the time.

Whether it be baseball, golf, fishing, skiing, driving, or turkey hunting, to do your best you must focus. Until a few years ago I had never heard the expression used as we do today, although I remember, as a boy, my father and more than one teacher ending my daydreaming with "Pay attention."

On Focus

My local area has had a spring turkey season for more than twenty years, but I could never enjoy it until I retired from the practice of veterinary medicine. May is the peak of foaling season, and most mares foal during the early-morning hours, right about the time a turkey hunter should be heading into the woods. There was no joy in turkey hunting for me, neither from the sights and sounds of the woods nor from the challenge of outwitting a smart old gobbler, when I had the gnawing guilt of being out of reach of the phone.

One of my hunting partners is a pharmacist, one of those rare individuals who owns his own store and keeps it open seven days a week serving our community. He loves the woods, hunting, and working his dogs as much as any person I know. Since his store doesn't open until 9 A.M. I could never understand why he would not go out at daylight and hunt spring turkeys when he could be back in time to go on duty. As I began to understand focus, though, I began to understand him. Unless he has a qualified substitute pharmacist so he can take a day off, he can't focus on hunting.

Conversely, being in the woods when you *can* bring yourself to focus on turkey hunting, and all the joy that goes with it, can ease your mind and help you forget cares that you can't do anything about; the kind of cares that keep you awake at night only to fade at sunrise are easily forgotten as you focus on turkey hunting. A beautiful sunrise, the song of a hermit thrush, the sight of a migrating warbler you have never seen before, or the delicate pink of an arbutus as you scrape away the leaves is a better tonic for a weary mind than any pharmaceutical, massage, or advice from a counselor. But — you must focus.

On Knowing the Territory

Even with all the modern hunting equipment, clothing, footwear, and high game populations we have available today, a hunter must be more skilled than when I was a teenager sixty years ago. The one thing my generation did have going for us was that as youngsters we were in the woods twelve months a year.

Adults had more free time, or at least fewer distractions, such as television, to take up their time. A greater proportion of the population lived in small towns or on farms, with familiar hunting territory close by. The professional and businesspeople in those country towns often owned an English setter or pointer and hunted grouse and pheasant.

In summer we youngsters hunted woodchucks; in fall, rabbits, squirrels, grouse, woodcocks, and pheasant. In winter we trapped muskrats, skunks, raccoons, and hoped for but seldom caught a mink or red fox. In late winter, if the snow was too deep for them to feed, we fed the pheasant down in the swamp. In spring we fished and caught frogs.

We never heard of scouting to check our hunting territory. It only consisted of a square mile or so, and we knew it well. We could say to a friend, "Meet me by the cold spring," or the three hickories, or Dean's ice pond, and he or she would know exactly where we meant. If a new fox den or a new coon tree was made in the area, we knew it just days after it happened. We knew each swale and each brush patch as well as the rabbits and pheasant that hid in them.

After World War II, when we were in our twenties, we didn't need to work two jobs and have a working spouse to support a family. We had more time, and more space to hunt. If we were going to hunt in strange territory, we wanted to know it well enough to be successful, so we took time to go and scout before the season, and "got to know the territory."

With today's lifestyle, young men and women in well-paying jobs work sixty-hour weeks; those on a lower pay scale work two jobs. Leisure time is scarce. If a person really wants to hunt and takes time off the first week of a season, those important first days are wasted unless he or she also managed to take off some days before the season to scout.

No matter how well you get to know a certain area over two or three seasons, you can't arrive at daylight the first day and be sure that game will be in the same place as previous years. Different crops in different fields, a late-spring frost causing a poor mast crop in fall, lumbering operations removing big trees but making new thick cover, new owners of neighboring property, and dozens of other factors can change the location of feeding, roosting, and hiding areas of all game, but particularly wild turkeys.

More hours spent on preseason scouting mean less hours needed to bag a turkey, and more enjoyment per hour of hunting. If you have to budget your time, increase scouting time, and shorten hunting.

Fall Scouting

I discussed scouting in the previous chapter, but just as fall hunting for wild turkeys is different from spring hunting, so, too, what you should look for and what you will see while scouting in fall is different from in spring. This difference is what we might in human terms call "the lifestyle" of the wild turkey.

Flock Size and Location

In spring mature toms live separately, and hen flocks are smaller. You will see jakes in pairs or small flocks of ten or more traveling together. In fall hens and their broods have started to flock up with other broods. By late fall Eastern wild turkey flocks of hens and their young poults of both sexes, along with hens of all ages, may contain hundreds of birds, sometimes incorrectly called droves. (*Droves* are groups of cattle or sheep.) Mature toms and yearling jakes will travel together in pairs, trios, and in flocks of up to a dozen or more, separate from the hen-and-poult flocks.

When the hard mast crop is plentiful and general, such as a good acorn year, flocks seem to stay smaller than when the food available is spotty or scarce. These smaller flocks of one to three broods will stay in the woods in such a year and are seldom seen in the open, creating the impression that the turkey numbers are way down. Conversely, when the mast crop is poor and the birds must feed on grass, grasshoppers, small seeds, fruit pits, wild grain, and cornfield waste, huge flocks seen in the open create an impression of overpopulation.

Because of the above facts, the general location of wild turkeys can be discovered some years by driving the roads or talking to people who travel country roads. In other years miles of walking may be necessary to locate fall birds. Even when you know the general location from road scouting, however, you'll need to do final scouting on foot to find the specific locations where hunting will be most successful.

Feeding Habits

Once they leave the roost in the morning and until they roost again at night, turkeys are constantly either eating or looking for food. When you walk around to scout, be on the watch not only for signs of where they have been — such as feathers, droppings, tracks, and scratchings — but also for food that they eat.

Turkeys seem to prefer a variety of foods, from grains and nuts to grass and grasshoppers. Here in the East about the only food they will stay on continually, with little else, is acorns.

The normal eating day for a flock might start with flying into a field where corn was just harvested. Next they will head for a hardwood forest, searching for acorns, beechnuts, and seedpods from ash trees. As they move through the forest they might find an occasional wintergreen or partridgeberry, or a salamander or earthworm. In old pastures and along stone walls and hedgerows they will find and feed on wild fruit, such as apples, wild cherries, and wild grapes. The same area may have a hickory with a few nuts that the squirrels haven't gotten. On a warm Indian summer afternoon they may next search an open hay field for grasshoppers, and eat clover or alfalfa before going back into the woods to roost. As these fall foods become more scarce watch for where cow manure, with its undigested corn content, is being spread.

As the scout you should find all these foods and catalog them in your mind, along with possible routes of entrance and egress. If you have time to watch an area you may see turkeys using these routes. Or you may find tracks in the mud where they cross a drainage ditch to reach a cornfield.

As you walk the woods differentiate between turkey scratchings, deer scrapings, squirrel diggings, and furrows where deer feed on beechnuts. See chapter 7 for details on these differences.

Just scouting the woods and back fields on an early-fall day can provide almost as much pleasure as hunting. As a bonus you may gather some late-summer flowers, such as New England asters, pick up some hickory, hazel-, or butternuts, taste wild apples to find a sweet one, or find a source of wintergreen, partridgeberries, and moss for a terrarium.

Finally, after a thorough job of scouting, you will see so much sign that the night before fall turkey season you won't sleep a wink. That's the way it should be, and is with me. When anticipation of the first day of the season doesn't keep me awake the night before, I will know I'm ready to quit hunting.

WINTERS LONG AGO

Have you wondered what wild turkeys ate during a hard winter three hundred years ago, when there was no corn-rich manure being spread? Ornithologists familiar with the history of the wild turkey write that since there were no roads or other man-made barriers to restrict their travel, wild turkeys simply migrated until they came to areas where winter food was available.

Classic Fall Hunt

One classically beautiful Indian summer morning I was "still hunting" along an upland ridge of abandoned pasture and mixed hardwoods with the excuse that I might put up a grouse or woodcock. If I saw and made a mental note of white-tailed deer sign, I'd consider it a bonus — just being there was all I really needed to be satisfied.

It was quieter walking in the pasture, with its soft grasses, sweet ferns, wild apples, and occasional shagbark hickory, than on the other side of the stone wall, where the ground was covered with noisy oak leaves. I'd walk a short distance, stop, look and listen, and wait, and then move on.

On occasion a flock of local wild geese, pushed off their ponds by Sunday-morning goose hunters, would sail honking just over my head, but out of range of my Ithaca Featherlight 16-gauge with its modified choke and #7½ shot.

In addition to the sound of the geese, I kept hearing what I thought was a small dog barking. Was it a very young beagle trying its voice on a rabbit, or was it a terrier farther away at one of the valley homes? Each time I moved forward and stopped, the sound seemed straight ahead on the far side of the stone wall.

Finally I saw something to match up with the sound. About a hundred yards away was a flock of wild turkeys, with a hen not much bigger than some of her brood. Other hunters were working the same ridge from another direction, and she was apparently trying to stay out of our way and keep her poults assembled around her.

We'd had a spring turkey season for several years, but not yet a fall season. I'd seen fall turkeys in the woods during deer season but, other than one flock years before, they were always scattered, perhaps by the presence of the deer hunters, and not in an organized flock with a hen giving the marching orders.

The flock seemed to just drift away and disappear into a brushy swamp ahead. As I thought about it, I remembered that I had heard that sound before but always assumed it was a small dog going "chup chup," a chipmunk with a deep voice, or a gray squirrel.

When the first fall turkey season came along, it made it possible for me to be in the woods and hunt turkeys when my practice was at its least demanding. Although fall hunting of wild turkeys is not considered as challenging as the spring hunt, for me there were many things in its favor (besides coming at a time when I could hunt without concern about foaling mares). Number one is that to many of us, fall is the time to hunt, spring is the time to fish. Second, a turkey bagged in fall, following the rules, is a trophy to be proud of. Challenge? Maybe not quite as much as a big spring tom, but still more than any other upland game in North America.

The Classic Technique

The classic fall hunt technique works best on smaller flocks, such as you may see in woods when food is plentiful. In theory, the technique involves temporarily breaking up the flock by shooting into a safe area and/or running toward them. Large flocks in open fields are more apt to just drift away in flock formation rather than disperse by flying in all directions.

You must then set up nearby and, after a period of silence, call using either the "kee kee kee" of the lost young turkey or the "chur chur chur" of the hen calling the flock in. Usually, the lead hen will try to assemble the flock by roosting time, but if a flock is broken up close to roosting time they may not respond to calling until sometime after daylight the next morning.

SAFETY TIP

Be careful where you shoot when scaring the flock; shotgun pellets can carry a long distance when shot high. When you shoot to scare the flock, shoot into the ground, somewhere between you and the flock.

Still Hunting

To put the theory into practice, you must first get close enough to a flock to really scare and disperse them, but not drive them as a flock too far away. The classic way is to still hunt through the woods, hoping to come within a hundred yards or so of a flock.

To succeed at still hunting you must be patient, alert, and focused. Different hunters have different methods of still hunting. Basically, it means walking quietly and slowly for a short distance, and then stopping to look and listen, such as animals and birds themselves do. Soft ground and wet leaves or snow increase your chances of seeing game. On dry days you need to vary your route so you can walk on moss or leaf-free grass, such as on a woods road. Following deer trails also permits you to move more silently.

Footwear should be soft soled, such as rubber pacs, that won't click on every stone you hit. Avoid canvas uppers that make a squeaking or scraping sound as one foot passes the other. Clothing should be soft so it will not make noise as you push past brush, and will not rustle as one leg passes the other, or when you raise your shotgun.

The most difficult part of still hunting is that although you must look to see where you place each step, you must constantly watch ahead and to the side as well. Develop a slow rhythm to your walk; place the foot that's going forward before you raise your other foot. Resist the temptation to cover a long distance — to "just reach the next high rise of ground to look off." As you get near a high point, stop only partway up, where you can peek over the rise.

Some still hunters, instead of steadily moving for fifty to one hundred yards between stops, will try to imitate the movements of deer by taking four or five steps, standing still for a few seconds, then moving again. This is considered a good technique when leaves are particularly dry and noisy.

When you do come on a flock of turkeys, they will generally be out of shotgun range, and you will usually have to shoot to scare them enough to make them disperse. Don't take the chance of wounding and losing one. Instead, unless one is within sure range with a clear head shot available, shoot into the ground between yourself and the flock. Then move to the

STILL HUNTING WITH A PARTNER

For a lone hunter to walk up on a flock of wild turkeys in the woods on a clear, dry day is in itself almost impossible, yet it can be done. The addition of a hunting partner adhering to a preagreed course and speed, with much patience, increases your chance to get close to a flock. Another hunter in the same area also increases the chance that while you are standing, birds moving away from him or her may come to within the correct distance for you to scare and disperse.

If you can team up with another hunter who is patient and enjoys still hunting, you both are fortunate. I recall boyhood friends who could move though the woods at the same slow pace that I did. We could work along on either side of a ridge, or through an alder swamp, and after several hours arrive at our preset destination, still at the proper safe distance apart and opposite each other.

approximate location where the center of the flock was, look for a big tree for a setup, and settle down.

Complete camouflage is just as necessary in fall hunting as spring. Remember that the slightest move or noise on your part will give you away. These fall birds may be only five months old, but they are every bit as wary as adults.

Wait for at least fifteen minutes to start calling. The waiting period may be an hour or more if the flock was seriously frightened. Use the "kee kee kee" of the lost young bird or the "chur chur chur" of the hen calling the flock to reassemble. As in spring hunting, don't call too much.

The birds usually come back as singles but may be in pairs or groups. If darkness comes before any come in, return the next morning to the approximate location and try again.

Whether you hunt alone or with partners, if you can develop your still hunting technique to a point where you often see game before it sees you, you will have learned an art of hunting that few people have the patience to master. In addition, you will derive more satisfaction from just being in the woods than many other hunters.

The turkey you shoot using the classic fall hunt technique may be only half the size of a good spring tom, but if you have followed all the rules you are still to be congratulated. To bag a wild turkey using the classic fall technique is not easy. In some ways it requires more skill and more work than the classic spring hunt. To me, still hunting is one of the most challenging, yet rewarding, styles of hunting. You can take pride that you succeeded where many with less patience, focus, and skill have failed. Just as important, you have on the young bird some of the finest-tasting meat available.

Fall Hunt Variations

On a warm and sunny October afternoon during the second year of fall wild turkey hunting in this area, my wanderings through the woods while still hunting brought me to the corner of a cornfield. The corn had been harvested two weeks earlier for silage, but in this corner that extended into the woods some had been knocked down by the tractor as it turned, pulling the chopper and wagon. I was tired and decided to sit a while with my back against a large white ash tree that, in years past, I had used as a place to sit and watch for deer.

Although during the first year of fall turkey hunting I had been able to fill my tag the classic way, breaking up a flock and calling a bird back, this year dry leaves and changed conditions had not allowed me to even come close. Deciding to sit and wait for the turkeys to come to me, I put on my mask, placed my old Ithaca Featherlight 16-gauge across my legs, and tried to be as still as possible.

With the warmth of the sun it wasn't long before I was dozing. How long I slept I have no idea, but I woke as though in a dream hearing turkey talk. Not daring to move, I just froze. The "churrup churrip" of the turkeys was to my right from the brushy edge of the field. With the late-afternoon sun shining directly into my eyes and the net mask over my glasses, it was difficult to see clearly into the field, where there appeared to be at least six turkeys, heads down, silently eating.

To my right, away from the sun, I could see and hear more birds coming through the brush, cautiously, with their heads up and ready to sound the alarm if I so much as moved my head or tried to raise my shotgun.

After what seemed an eternity, all of the turkeys came into the field and began to eat. Still, through the glare of the sun there always seemed to be at least one with its head up. Finally, when all the heads seemed to be down I raised my shotgun, determined that I would shoot at the first head that came up. Trying to peer through the scope, I was again frustrated. With the bright sun I could see nothing.

What to do? There I was with at least a dozen turkeys within twenty yards, but with the bright sun hitting the front of my scope I was blind. Again I waited, shotgun raised and pointed, but unable to find a clear target to shoot at.

As so often happens when hunting, when things happen they happen so fast you react by instinct. One second all the birds were eating; the next I heard a "puck! puck!" as one detected me. What appeared to be the whole flock dashed for the brush, giving me no clear shot.

Then to my far left a lone straggler took to the air, flew by me, and sailed, curving to my right, above the brush. With the sun behind me, I followed her with the scope, placed the crosshairs ahead of her outstretched head, and, still following, squeezed off. Her trail continued sloping downward into the brush for another twenty feet.

When I picked her up, it was obvious she wouldn't weigh over seven pounds dressed. Still, my heart was going top speed, and as I walked across the field with her over my shoulder, she got heavier and heavier.

At Thanksgiving, when my family took the wild turkey in preference to the supermarket bird, I was convinced it had been worth it to sit, listen, watch, and wait.

What I learned about wild turkeys that sunny October day was basically what you must know to be able to successfully hunt them in fall using the most usual variation from the classic fall hunt. First and foremost, I learned that wild turkeys are constantly on the alert for danger. With their acutely sensitive hearing and keen eyesight, they notice any movement or sound that is not natural to their surroundings. When a hen gives the "puck! puck!" warning, they are either going to just fade away out of shotgun range, start running, or, if necessary, explode into flight. Second, I learned that you must learn to wait.

To Sit, Listen, Watch, and Wait

The most common variation from the classic fall hunt — using calling to hunt fall turkeys — combines concealment, listening, watching, and waiting.

The term most often used to describe the process of sitting in concealment and waiting for your prey is *ambush*, but that carries a bad connotation — human hunting human, being sneaky, hiding in the bushes, and all that. Deer hunters don't use the word *ambush*, they hunt from a "stand." Whether it be a platform in a tree or a seat on a stump, the hunt is still conducted "on stand." Waterfowl hunters hunt from a "blind."

Even the spring gobbler hunter conceals himself in camouflage and, hiding at his setup, ambushes the tom coming in to his call. I do wish there was a more accepted word to describe it. Perhaps we could use the word *sit* — that is, to "sit at our setup waiting for a turkey or turkeys to appear."

If you have scouted properly, you know where turkeys are feeding and where they travel to reach these feeding spots. Your first choice for a place to set up and sit should be along their travel routes. A good second would be in woods near the edge of a field where they are feeding.

Although it may be legal to shoot a turkey while it is in a tree, it isn't always the correct thing to do. It is difficult to tell the sex of a turkey high over your head in a tree. In a "toms-only" hunt you could make a lawbreaking mistake. Further, shooting a turkey from that angle will damage a large portion of breast meat and/or puncture intestines, damaging the whole carcass.

It does not seem quite sporting to sit directly under a roosting area or, in a dry part of the country, to set up near a water supply. If you kill birds in these places the survivors may relocate miles away, completely out of the area.

Location of your setup is important. It must be where you can conceal yourself and, ideally, where turkeys will pass by you from side to side, not suddenly come in from behind and surround you. If they pass from side to side at about fifteen to twenty yards away, you have half a chance to look them over and pick out one of the larger birds. Shooting the *largest* bird in such a flock isn't the wisest choice, since this will probably be the hen. First, it doesn't seem right to take a brood-producing hen, and second, one of this year's birds with her will make much better eating. If they do come in from behind you, the first birds are often the smallest, and are so close that they'll see your slightest move. In such a situation you rarely get a shot.

Regardless of where they come from, you will more likely hear them before you see them. A flock of young birds with hens will make a

Fall is a great time to start a youngster. At twelve years of age, Joe got these two birds from a tom and jake flock by sitting, listening, watching, and waiting. Joe says, "Hunting is more fun than baseball."

musical, high-pitched "churrup churrip," but you may also hear the lower-toned "chup chup" of the hens. A flock of jakes makes a medium-pitched, short, often single "churrp." A flock of jakes and toms, or toms only, makes little sound, but sometimes a "pluck" or almost a "kluck." When you do hear them, if your face covering is not in place or your shotgun is pointed in the wrong direction, it is too late to change anything. All you can do is freeze and hope they don't hear your pounding heart or your breath.

> ### KNOW THE LAW
>
> Many states and provinces, but not all, permit birds of either sex to be shot in fall, and more than one per day. You must be familiar with local regulations before you hunt to avoid making serious law-breaking blunders.

In late fall when flocks have become large — literally hundreds of birds feeding on cornfield waste or the corn from manure spread on fields — shooting at the birds doesn't seem to make them leave the general area, as happens in early fall with smaller flocks. If birds are seen in these areas near roosting time and are undisturbed, they often come sailing out into these fields at daylight.

In such a situation it is best to let them come and settle down to feed before shooting. In this way you can take your pick — or, if the law requires toms only, you can pick out a red head and beard. Further, if you are hunting with partners, wait until enough birds are down, and spread out so everyone gets a shot.

A Still Hunting Variation

The art and technique of still hunting was described under "Classic Fall Hunt." However, in a variation from the classic fall hunt you may get close enough to a wild turkey, or wild turkey flock, to bag a bird without dispersing them and calling them back. Or you may hear turkey sounds, quietly set up, and start calling, trying to imitate the sounds you hear. On occasion a curious bird may respond, or a lone tom or jake looking for company may come in.

For someone of my nature who enjoys walking as well as hunting, still hunting gives a sense of satisfaction even if I bag no game. It is rare that an hour or two of still hunting does not reward with a memorable sight — a fisher chasing a squirrel, a sunning raccoon sleeping off the effects of too many wild grapes, or a witch hazel bush with its seedpods exploding seeds from the cold while its branches are already in bloom with next year's yellow blossoms.

Decoys for Fall Turkey Hunting

Much of what I said about the use of decoys for spring wild turkey hunting also applies to using decoys in fall.

The use of decoys for the classic fall hunt seems a little cumbersome, even with the new lightweight models. But if you're so inclined, you may well increase your chances of luring a bird into range.

Decoys are of value if set in a field where birds have fed on previous days, to make them less wary when coming out to feed. In such a situation you may put the decoy, or preferably decoys, out of range of your setup. Your setup, however, should be along the trail where you believe the birds will be coming. More than one hunter with more than one setup covering all possible entry routes is ideal and justifies the use of several decoys.

SAFETY TIP

In fall season, especially in areas where birds of either sex may be taken, be extremely careful about where you position your decoy and setup. Be sure that another hunter mistaking the decoy for a live bird will have to come out into the open and be seen by you before shooting toward you.

Use of Rifles

Hunting regulations in few states and provinces permit the use of rifles for hunting wild turkeys. Because rifles allow you to shoot from a much greater distance, it's especially important that they're used only where the range is open and where there is little cover to hide the hunter or the hunted. Check with your local game commission for regulations on the use of rifles for hunting turkeys.

Expanding bullets of calibers used for large game destroy a large portion of meat. In chapter 5 I discussed rifles and ammunition that are considered suitable for use in turkey hunting. These are mainly in the .22-caliber range, with nonexpanding bullets and extreme accuracy.

Since hitting a turkey in the head while using a rifle is difficult, and hitting the body destroys so much meat, a compromise is to aim low in the neck region, just ahead of the breast. As with any gun, however, experience gives you the greatest insight into its range and capability.

HUNTING WITH A MUZZLELOADER

Next to hunting turkeys with a bow, I can't think of a greater challenge than using a muzzleloader. To be sure, our ancestors used them to hunt turkeys with good results — or bad, if you consider that they nearly exterminated them. Accounts of the Lewis and Clark expedition, 1804–06, mention wild turkeys as one of the most desirable species of game killed for food.

For more information on using muzzleloaders to hunt turkeys, see pages 45–47. If you are looking for a challenge, turkey hunting with a muzzleloader is, without a doubt, one of the best.

Driving

Hunting by driving is done by two groups of hunters. The "drivers," or "beaters," work through a cover where the game is hidden in the hope of driving the game out to another group, the "standers," "watchers," or "shooters."

In areas like western Massachusetts, where deer hide in thick cover, such as laurel, this technique is regularly used with success. A few drivers can move a whole herd of deer.

As for turkeys, in such thick cover it would take a whole flock of men to drive one turkey. Besides, the practice is dangerous, since the only time the drivers or watchers see the turkeys is when they take to the air. Shooting a modern turkey shotgun at a flying turkey when the exact location of other hunters is not known can bring fatal results.

Two or more hunters still hunting an area is not considered driving. A flock may move away from one hunter to within range of another, but they are not being "driven."

Game regulations in some states list driving as one of the illegal ways of hunting turkeys. Even if it's legal, I don't think it should ever be considered as a sporting way to hunt.

DON'T STALK!

Don't even think about stalking wild turkeys! Crawling, inching along on your abdomen, or darting from cover to cover in full camouflage after wild turkeys that some other hunter may also be watching is a foolish risk of your own life, and could ruin the life of the hunter who mistakes the movement in the bushes for a turkey.

I have hunted with friends who have bagged toms by just getting a little closer by stalking, and I have been tempted a few times to try it myself. However, turkey hunting accident reports all point to the utter stupidity of the practice. One of my hunting buddies called in not a turkey, but an eleven-year-old boy, one morning. My friend never got closer to shooting than releasing the safety, and he spoke to the boy before getting shot himself, but still remembers it as a bad dream.

Hunting Turkeys with Dogs

Turkeys were not on my mind as I started to hike up the jeep trail to my cabin at 9 A.M. one frosty October morning in 1986. I was thinking about the few hours of work I had to do to make the cabin ready for winter, although since it was fall turkey season I carried my Ithaca Mag 10 on its sling with the idea of hunting on my way down in the afternoon. With my hands free to grab a sapling as needed, I was planning to start straight up the steep mountainside, shortcutting the switchbacks of the jeep trail. With me was Bert, my thirteen-month-old yellow Lab.

The jeep trail is a series of switchbacks, going about six-tenths of a mile to climb half that distance through black birches and hemlocks to an open mountain meadow where, with some help from family and two friends, I had built a Swiss-style one-room cabin during the summer.

As we prepared to leave the jeep trail before the first switchback, turkeys began leaving the trees and sailing up the mountain. This was a surprise. Although I have known turkeys to roost in the hemlocks along the trail, up until this time I didn't know that when well fed, a flock will linger until midmorning before flying down.

Bert started to go up toward them, but I called him back, and with him at heel we dropped back to the trail and continued around the switchback.

Bert had a bit of experience searching for and retrieving released chukar partridge, but other than "stay" and "heel" hadn't had much training. With his puppylike exuberance he didn't always follow even these basic commands. Still, from hunting and retrieving parentage, he showed good potential.

Bert ignored rabbits, squirrels, cats, and all other four-footed creatures, and was interested only in things that flew or smelled to him like something that would fly. On our evening walks, if a low-flying plane went over he would watch it until it was out of sight. His vacuumlike nose checked every hedgerow. When he smelled bird his tail would rotate like a propeller.

My hope for Bert was that he would become my grouse-hunting companion for my retirement years, as a pointer-setter cross named Spotty had been in my boyhood. We had named him Bert hoping he would be at least half as good a dog as our beloved eighty-five-year-old attorney named Bert was a man. The thought of a dog trained to use on wild turkeys never entered my mind until after this day's adventure.

As we came around the switchback to the next level Bert started sniffing the edge of the trail and his tail went into rotary motion. I unslung the Mag 10 and peered into the brushy woods looking for turkeys, but felt sure they were long gone, either farther up the mountain or along the slope directly away.

Suddenly, a red head popped up not over thirty yards away. With my crosshairs just over the red head I fired. The head disappeared, but I could see the flopping of wings. I told Bert, "Find him, Bert," as I would had I shot at a chukar that he was being trained on.

Bert tore through the brush toward the flopping bird, but much to my disappointment veered off to the left down the hill. With my shotgun on safety I ran to the flopping bird, calling to Bert to come back. I stood over the bird still calling for Bert to come back. Then I spotted him fifty yards down the hill with the head of another turkey in his mouth, and both front legs and his chest holding the turkey down. I picked up the dying jake and ran to Bert. The turkey he was holding was wounded but still very much alive. She was too big for Bert to retrieve, but she sure wasn't going anywhere with one hundred pounds of yellow Lab holding her down.

As is true with most adventures, I learned a lot that October morning. First, during early fall turkeys may stay on the roost until midmorning or beyond. Second, no matter how careful you are when shooting at the head of one fall turkey, you might wound a second one you don't even see. Third, with wild turkeys, as with all bird hunting, a dog will find cripples and lost birds. Fourth, I had broken the one-bird limit law and had to find a friend with a tag. And fifth, there seemed to be a real future in the use of dogs in fall turkey hunting.

I wish I could say that I went on and continued Bert's training so that he became a perfect turkey dog. Particularly today, with more turkeys around and no more one-fall-bird restriction, a well-trained retriever would be a fine asset to turkey hunting. I have used him to find wounded birds on two occasions, but never worked on him to find and break up flocks, and then "stay" at the setup while I sat and tried to call turkeys back.

I do believe that, as years go by and younger people with fresh ideas about turkey hunting come along, turkey dogs will become more common.

The hunting strain of Labrador retriever should make the ideal turkey dog. Black and chocolate would seem easier to hide when sitting on setup, but a net camouflage cover could easily be made for a yellow or light-colored dog. Any bird dog breed should be good enough to find and break up flocks, but it takes firmness and training by the owner to have a dog return to "heel" and "stay" after seeing those big birds fly.

Over the years I've known bird hunters who would lose all interest in hunting if they didn't have a dog to work. If you feel fall turkey hunting lacks something and it is legal in your state or province, why not add a dog?

After breaking up a flock a well-trained dog will wait while the hunter tries to call in individual birds.

After the Hunt: From Bleeding to Butchering

A cold wet spring can mean many unbred hens still roosting with toms late in hunting season and difficulty for the hunter trying to separate them. One such year, even when I followed the time-honored tactic of locating the approximate site of a roosting tom by his evening gobble and being near his tree early the next morning, I found that my calling was to no avail. Few turkey hunters are skilled enough to call a tom to them when he has a real live hen with him. Not being one of those few, my tom would fly down and, after one or two gobbles, go off with his harem.

The advice of a more skilled hunter on such a situation was, "Go home, have a good breakfast, and go back out to near that location about ten. By that time the tom will have bred any hen nearby, had his breakfast, and be on the lookout for a new hen."

The last day of the season, still having one unfilled tag and a desire for one last hunt, I followed the skilled hunter's advice. Ten o'clock found me at the edge of some woods that surrounded a long, narrow, recently plowed field. The previous evening I had heard several gobbles in the woods behind me, and knew there had been turkeys in the area all spring. I found a big black oak for a backrest and set up.

The woods were quiet as far as turkeys were concerned, but every other sort of bird and numerous insects made their presence known. After about fifteen minutes I worked my slate to give as good an imitation of a hen looking for a tom as possible. Almost immediately my call was answered from across the field, which seemed to me to be ideal, because he'd have to come out in the open to reach my well-hidden setup.

For thirty minutes he gobbled on and off, and from time to time I saw him strutting just on the edge of the woods on the far side of the field. With not much more than an hour left to hunt, I tried a desperate move — I went up the hill behind me, along the side of the hill, staying in the woods all around the field to end up at an angle behind and to the right of the gobbler.

Again I set up, with only a half hour to hunt, tried a call on my little box plunger call, and waited. This time I heard an answer from my left, close to where I felt the tom I'd been working had been earlier. The rolling contour of the field left a blind spot on a portion of where the tom had strutted before, but if he came a bit farther he'd be in view and in range.

There were no more gobbles but I thought I could hear the sighlike "whoosha whoosh" of a strutting gobbler to my left.

Then there he was, just his head and neck, staring at me with one eye. I froze, hoping he wouldn't see my eyes blink. After a few seconds he was gone. Had he made me out and disappeared?

Again I heard the "whoosha whoosh." He was still there! Five minutes later his head and neck appeared and again I froze, cursing myself for not having my gun up. As before, he vanished and five minutes later I heard another "whoosha whoosh."

This time I raised the shotgun, waiting without much hope for what seemed like forever. The gun barrel rotated as my arms got tired, but I still kept it up there at the ready.

Just as I was about to give up, deciding it was all over, there he was staring at me from fifty yards. The only movement I had to make was to squeeze the trigger, which I did. He dropped out of sight.

Standing up, I could see him lying there without even a visible quiver. I put the safety on the gun and ran to him through the mud of the plowed field. Not wanting to put my

SAFETY TIP

After shooting at a turkey, put your safety on your gun before you start running toward it. Once you have the bird in your control, with your foot on both its legs and your gun in a safe place, it is a good idea to slip on a blaze orange vest over your camouflage. Models made of light nylon are available and take up very little room in your pocket or pack.

shotgun down in the mud, I reached down to grab his legs but got hold of only one.

At the same instant he went into motion with both wings and his free leg. Seconds later it was all over, but the one-inch spur on his free leg did a job on my arm and wristwatch. The arm healed in a few days, but the watch was totaled, with the hands reading 11:56, four minutes before the season closed.

This bird weighed twenty-three pounds, far heavier than any other I have ever shot. Later, when I dressed him, I found that one #4 pellet had gone clean through his head and several more had gone through his neck. I assume the one through the head had found his brain and accounted for his dropping, and the sudden activity was his death struggle.

As a veterinarian I am well aware that it is possible to be kicked by a dead horse, but now I also know that it is foolhardy to grab one leg on a dying tom turkey.

Bleeding

Properly shot birds, with pellets in the neck and head, perhaps bleed well enough. However, if at all possible, try to bleed them more by using your jackknife. For your own safety, place one of your feet on both the bird's legs and grab the bird's head with one hand, with the back of his head in your palm. With your knife open his mouth and pierce up and back through the cleft in the roof of his mouth, trying to hit the brain. If not already dead, the bird will shudder as you pith the brain. Then retract the knife and, pushing the blade back into the throat, cut left and right to sever the large blood vessels. Lift the bird by the legs, head down, and let him bleed. Thorough bleeding improves meat quality.

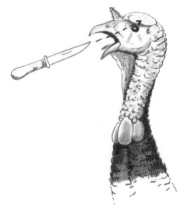

Now, if you haven't already been able to do so, put on your orange vest and unload your shotgun. Take your bird back to your setup. If you are a pipe smoker, load your pipe, sit down, and relax. If the law requires, fill out your tag and/or license. Have a sip of coffee from your thermos, or a candy bar. Pick up around your setup, but above all, relax!

A bird immediately pithed after shooting will dry pick easier than if allowed to die slowly.

Field Dressing

During warm weather it is perhaps a wise idea to eviscerate your bird immediately in the field. Whether you do it now or after you completely pluck the bird, the procedure is the same:

1. Pluck feathers from around the anus to the bottom of the tail; to the top of the keel, or breastbone; and almost out to each leg. With the bird on its back and the blade of your knife facing up, make a cut as wide as your knife under the breast-bone.

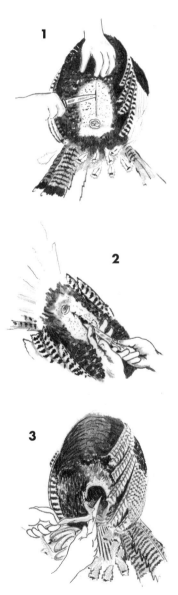

2. With your knife blade facing out and your fingers guiding the cut from behind, cut down toward the anus, being careful not to puncture the intestines.

3. If clean water is available, wet your hand before reaching in with the back of your hand against the inside of the breastbone, going as far forward as possible, and scoop out the whole mass, or at least the intestines. (Lung tissue between the ribs and kidney on the roof of the abdominal cavity may be scooped out, or left for removal at home.) With the intestines out and the anus still attached, cut around the anus and discard the intestines. Coyotes, foxes, and bobcats will clean these up overnight.

4. After removing the abdominal cavity contents, you still have the crop to deal with. This is better handled at home, after plucking, by removing the bird's head and sliding the neck skin back, which may

require slitting and removing the neck as close as possible to the body. (The neck, if not too badly shot up, may then be saved for soup.) Following the gullet, reach into the forward body cavity and find the crop — easily done if full, but difficult if empty. Peel it out and discard.

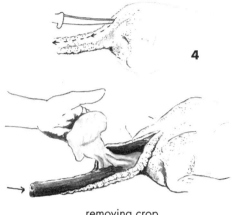

removing crop

Don't be alarmed if the crop on a mature spring gobbler is surrounded by a brownish yellow, almost decayed-appearing fat. This is normal in spring toms, difficult to remove, and will be discussed further under "Butchering."

Plucking

If you don't have a bragging-size bird that you want to show off, and if hunting regulations permit it, in warm weather you might just as well pluck the bird right in the field. Where required, leave the beard as evidence of sex.

The sooner after killing, the easier the feathers pluck and the quicker the carcass cools. Still, even a ten-pounder slung over your shoulder with his tail spread as you walk across an open field to your truck makes you feel like he's twice that big.

SAVING THE GIBLETS

Liver, heart, and gizzard should be saved if not shot damaged. Trim the gall bladder from the liver; empty the gizzard by cutting and tearing out the wrinkled inside sac. Place these giblets in a plastic bag to be further trimmed and cleaned where you have clean water.

How to Pluck

Regardless of where you pluck, get to it as soon as possible.

1. Hold the bird by his neck and start plucking *a few feathers at a time* over the breast. Pull in the same direction as the feathers lie. You will soon develop the motion — you sort of push feathers back into the skin and then, with a quick little snap, they are out. After getting started you may find it easier and more comfortable to hang the bird by his legs while you pluck the rest.

2. Avoid tearing skin on shot-damaged birds by holding the edge of the wound and taking only a feather or two at a time.

3. If you are going to save tails and/or wings, read the box on page 112 before proceeding. Otherwise, pluck over the whole bird rapidly

Plucking is easier if the bird is suspended by its legs, freeing up both your hands to work.

and then go back and get what you missed. Wing and tail feathers may need to be pulled one at a time.

4. Young fall birds in particular are apt to be full of tiny black pinfeathers. These need to be pulled one at a time, with a knife, holding the feather to your thumb. You may have to resort to removing pinfeathers under cool running water. Scalding or chilling with or without paraffin (see below) may also help.

Scalding

On occasion you may find a bird that you just can't pluck dry. Rather than tear the skin or, worse yet, resort to skinning, these birds can be plucked easily by scalding. Water must be heated to 135°F in a container large enough to cover the turkey. Depending on size, dip the bird in for thirty-five to forty-five seconds, raising it up and down so that the water works in around the feathers. All but wing and tail feathers can then be removed easily.

Using Paraffin

If, after plucking, hair or a lot of small feathers remain, you can make a better-looking carcass by using paraffin.

Chill the bird and dip for a few seconds in a pail of water that has two or three quarter-pound pieces of paraffin melted and floating on top. The paraffin will harden, and when peeled off will take most unwanted feathers, hair, and debris with it.

Is It Worth It?

Plucking may sound like a lot of tedious work, but it really isn't that bad. I was amused at an article on food used at the first Thanksgiving in which the author said that the original wild turkeys were so covered with ticks that they were skinned before cooking. I would guess that this was a misinterpretation of the Colonial script, which described those nasty little black pinfeathers. Once you have tasted a young fall turkey properly prepared, you will not mind the time it takes to remove them.

Butchering

As soon as possible after plucking, run cold water over and through your turkey. While doing this you should try to remove the remains of the lung tissue from between the ribs, and the kidney tissue high in the abdominal cavity under the back. Remove the beard to dry. On older birds you may

SAVING THE TAIL OR WINGS FOR MOUNTING

If you wish to save the tail or wings, you must proceed carefully as you pluck. To save a tail for mounting you need to avoid losing the beautiful bronze-striped feathers ahead of the tail. Do this by skinning from a third of the way up the back down to the tail. Then cut the tail off. To save a wing for mounting you must cut it off. Procedures for mounting wings and tails are discussed in chapter 10.

POSING YOUR TROPHY FOR A PICTURE

Study pictures you see of hunters with wild turkeys. For your own photo, concentrate on what you want to show. Smooth the feathers and remove any blood, mud, or burrs.

Just holding the bird by his legs does not really show the tail as most people would like, although a side view on a really good bird with a long beard is worth a try. It always seems as though you need a third hand to spread the tail and hold the bird, but with a little patience it can be done. Sitting on a hassock-size box or kneeling will allow you to show

Kneeling behind the turkey puts you in a good position not only to fan the tail feathers but also to be captured in the photo yourself.

off your bird's tail spread. Poses with the tail spread so that the undersides of the tail feathers show are more difficult than from the top side. Take some shots with the head curled back almost out of sight, so it doesn't look too grotesque, and some with it in plain sight.

Pictures of you carrying the bird slung over your back can be great if you are careful about background. Green leaves tend to dominate the picture if you are trying to make it look real. You'll get better results if the trees have not yet leafed out.

You can take advantage of the background, particularly in fall, by showing the bird carried over your shoulder with some beautiful scenery in the distance. For more about field photography, see chapter 11.

A SPECIAL SOUP

Many deer hunters follow the tradition of removing the tenderloin from the recently butchered deer and preparing it as a special treat with biscuits and coffee. The turkey giblets and neck, particularly of young fall-killed birds, make a wonderful, tasty soup that may be served within hours of butchering. This has become a tradition in our family. To prepare the soup, place the neck and giblets in enough water to cover; add a handful of rice, salt and pepper to taste, one stalk of celery, chopped, and one small onion, chopped. Simmer for an hour or until rice is cooked.

want to save the legs with the spurs. If you have a vise or pipe vise you may be able to clamp the leg in it, cut around the joint, and, by pulling and bending, remove the leg tendons from the turkey's thigh.

The carcass of a turkey damaged by shot should be trimmed of all bloody, damaged tissue. In some rare cases this could mean complete skinning and boning, saving only the damage-free meat. (Boning techniques are described on page 116.)

If you saved the liver, gizzard, and heart, you should wash them in cold running water to clean and cool them. If not already done in the field, open the gizzard to remove the contents, and peel the crinkled, hard lining. The smooth inner lining of the gizzard should also be trimmed off. The giblets and neck should then be put in the refrigerator.

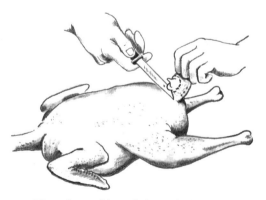

If you have skinned the turkey's back to save its feathers, you already may have removed the oil gland.

The water-cooled carcass should then be put in ice water for a few hours. After ice-water chilling you will be better able to remove the brownish yellow fat from the breast cavity of the mature spring tom. This is sometimes easier said than done, but possible with patience and a small sharp knife. This cavity makes an excellent space for more dressing when roasting. Before refrigerating the chilled carcass, also remove the oil gland just under the skin ahead of the tail. If you skinned this area to save tail feathers, you may have already accomplished this.

If properly refrigerated, a fresh turkey can be kept for up to a week before cooking.

Freezing Your Turkey

The carcass should be refrigerated for twenty-four hours before drying and wrapping to freeze. Freezing will take place faster if the carcass is wrapped in one layer of plastic until frozen through, and then wrapped with freezer paper or brown paper bags. Use double or triple wrapping over the initial plastic. Adequate wrapping will protect against freezer burn, extend the possible storage time, and give you better-tasting meat.

If properly bled, field dressed, plucked, chilled, frozen, and wrapped, a turkey should be good for at least six months. After that it may lose some flavor from freezer burn and drying, but will still be edible for another three to four months.

FILLETING THE BREAST

To fillet a turkey breast you need a sharp thin-bladed knife. With the skinned, partially skinned, or unskinned bird on his back, stand to the rear and, if you are right handed, cut along the breastbone on the bird's left side. Separate the meat from the bone with care, following the contour of the bone, leaving as little flesh on the bone as possible. You should be able to come up with a filletlike piece of breast. Now, if it seems handier, turn the bird around and bone the bird's right breast.

Boning

In a couple of instances you will need to bone your turkey. As mentioned earlier, you may need to bone shot-damaged birds to salvage undamaged portions. Also, if you would like to try smoking your turkey, you will have better results if you at least partially bone it.

Although I don't generally recommend skinning turkeys, boned or partially boned breasts are usually skinned before processing. Wings and legs may be smoked with skin on, but they will need a little longer in the presmoking salting mixture in relation to their weight. Make adjustments as necessary.

1. To remove a complete breast, lift the breast up with one hand while you cut with a sharp knife or poultry shears to separate the breast from the rest of the carcass.
2. If not shot damaged, legs and wings may be removed from the carcass at the joint closest to the body and prepared as separate pieces, or smoked if you desire.
3. Boning the rest of the carcass is done either by cutting as much meat from the bones as possible, or by boiling the whole carcass to loosen the meat and then separating it. (The fresh bones make good additions to the giblets or soup.)

Uncooked meat may be ground to make turkey patties, turkey sausage, or turkey meat loaf. If you do not wish to cook it immediately, it may be frozen in one- or two-pound packages and stored for up to three months. Be sure to allow enough time to thaw the meat in the refrigerator or in cold water. Boiled, boned meat may be used for turkey pie, tetrazzini, or other dishes. See chapter 12 for a variety of recipes.

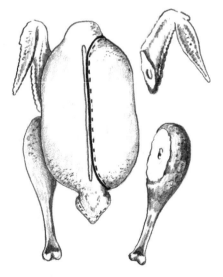

Cut as close to the bone as possible to save all the breast meat in one piece. The bones with remaining meat should be used for soup.

Smoking Turkey

Turkey is smoked to give it a distinctive flavor, not to prolong its storage time. In no way should it be confused with smoked meats, such as "jerky," or with Virginia-style smoked pork hams or Norwegian-style smoked venison, which may be stored without refrigeration for months.

Turkey breasts, boned or partially boned, and other body parts can be lightly pickled (salted, corned) and then smoked. Salted smoked turkey can then be cooked and frozen, but its storage time is less than that of fresh meat because of its high water content.

Salting

To salt your own turkey cuts you may purchase commercial salt mixtures, or you can make your own brine using a mixture of the following ingredients:

> **9 pounds clean rock salt or water softener salt**
> **3 pounds sugar**
> **3 ounces saltpeter**
> **4 quarts drinking-quality water**

1. Place the salt, sugar, and saltpeter (this may be difficult to obtain, and can be left out) in a clean, sanitized earthen crock, stainless-steel tub, or good-quality plastic garbage can. Pour in the water — it should be hot — and dissolve the mixture by stirring. Don't be discouraged if some of the salt does not dissolve completely.
2. After it cools, check the strength of the brine by using a hydrometer. You can also rely on the farmer's method of trying to float an egg on the water. If the brine is concentrated enough, the egg will float with just a bit of its shell above the water's surface. If it sinks, you need to add more salt.
3. With the temperature of the brine at 40°F, immerse the meat. You may have to weigh it down with a clean stone to keep it covered with the brine mixture. The container with its contents should be kept at 36 to 40°F during processing. If the temperature is lower, increase the time; if it goes above 40°F, put ice in watertight plastic and place it in the brine.
4. Try salting times of 6 hours for small skinless breasts and up to 9 hours or more for whole breasts. Soaking times for legs, wings, and other parts will fall somewhere in between.
5. After salting, dry the meat and hang it at 40°F to further dry for 24 to 48 hours prior to smoking.

Smoking Techniques

Smoking is done more for flavor than for drying, so use cool smoke. Small factory-made smokers tend to run hot but may be used with discretion. If you do not have a smokehouse, you may construct one with a fifty-five-gallon drum, a few lengths of stovepipe, and a five-gallon metal pail as a "firebox." The longer the stovepipe, the cooler the smoke.

There is pride and satisfaction in salting and smoking your own meat.

Hickory, apple, and even corncobs or a mixture of the three make good smoke. If you don't have much smoking experience, try smoking with no meat in the smokehouse until you are satisfied that you can maintain steadily cool, sweet-smelling smoke. Don't be afraid to experiment and use your imagination, varying salt mixtures, salting times, and smoking times. Try some sweet fern stems on your smoke fire and, if available, such woods as mesquite. Surprise your friends with your own unique smoked turkey flavor.

SMOKING TIMES

Try a twelve-hour smoking time for small half breasts, wings, or legs, and then taste your results. You may need to increase to sixteen hours or more for larger pieces.

Preserving Your Trophy

There are two fish and game clubs in this local area. Both have comfortable lodges, where members may enjoy club functions such as clambakes, barbecues, game dinners, and pig roasts. Sometimes a family celebrating a wedding anniversary or a "gathering of the clan," or an organization without it own lodge, will use the facilities for a function, such as a turkey shoot.

It is always interesting to walk around these lodges and look at the trophies. There are beautiful white-tailed deer mounts, some going back fifty years and some of recent vintage. Also, of course, pictures were taken in good years when many carcasses hung from the meat pole.

Of more interest, however, are the wild turkey trophies. Most of these were done by the hunters themselves, using materials at hand. There is great ingenuity shown in creating a display of not only tails but also tails and beards; in a few cases, tails, beards, spurs; and in one really interesting one, tail, beard, and legs.

I'm sure every one of these has a story, but turkey hunters like to talk about the really smart old beard dragger that made a fool of everyone and is still off there on Ox Bow Mountain, surrounded by his harem, gobbling his defiance.

Do It Yourself or Get Professional Help?

A full-body mount of a wild turkey is impressive, not just in appearance but also in size. Although few people will want one to display in their home because of this size, if you are one of the few, you want him to look as though he is still alive, the way you remember him when he appeared in front of you. Certainly every game club and hunting lodge in wild turkey areas should have one.

A full-body mount certainly requires a professional taxidermist, and not just any taxidermist, either. Other parts, such as tail, wings, beards, and spurs, can be done by any hunter with a little time, patience, and attention to detail. Those made by a professional may be more perfect and more durable, yet the satisfaction of doing it yourself is all part of the turkey hunting mystique.

I'll first describe what preparations you must make in order to have a full-body mount to be proud of. Then I'll tell you how to save beards, wings, spurs, legs, and feet, before discussing the way most hunters make tail mounts. I'll also describe in detail a method of mounting the full-spread tail of the wild turkey in such a way that it will be durable, attractive, and clean enough so that you can hang it in any room in your home.

Preparing for a Full-Body Mount

Few toms are perfect enough in size, stature, and measurements to deserve a full-body mount. Still, you cannot wait until that perfect bird lays dying before you to decide that "this is the one."

If you have any idea that you might someday want to have a whole turkey mounted, start locating taxidermists in the area you hunt and compare their qualifications. Price should be your last consideration. The best- and the least-qualified taxidermists probably charge about the same, which has to be a lot because of the time and skill required. Your main consideration should be a quality mount and the taxidermist who best can provide you with it.

The National Wild Turkey Federation can give you some advice on qualified taxidermists. Still, if you go into a taxidermist's studio and see mounts he or she is doing for customers that look good, why go farther?

When that perfect bird does fall to your shot, don't break his neck and don't let him lie flopping, which will knock good feathers out of his wings and tail. Grab him by both legs and hold his head down until he dies.

Once the tom is no longer flopping and obviously dead, smooth his feathers. If he did lose a tail or wing feather, retrieve it. *Do not eviscerate.*

If you have far to carry him to transportation, take off an article of your clothing, such as a T-shirt or turtleneck, and slide it over his body from head to tail.

If at all possible, drive him directly to the taxidermist. In

SAFETY TIP

Put some blaze orange on the turkey when you're carrying him out of the field or woods.

warm weather, if there is to be a delay of more than three hours, put a plastic bag over him to keep him dry, then pack ice around him. If the delay will be days, phone the taxidermist and see what he thinks about freezing the whole bird.

Saving Individual Parts

If you don't want the expense of a professional full-body mount, try saving the bird's beard, wings, spurs, legs, or feet.

Saving a Beard

Most times you can remove a turkey's beard by grasping it close to the body and simply pulling it loose from the skin. For a real trophy — one that you don't want to damage — pull it until you have it a bit away from the body and cut it off with a sharp knife, taking a bit of the turkey's skin with it.

A third method — for a beard you want to display in an unusual manner — is to remove skin and feathers in a three-inch-diameter circle with the beard in the middle.

Beards themselves will dry without spoiling, but if you remove a circle of skin, it must be refrigerated, frozen, or immediately treated with salt and/or borax to preserve it.

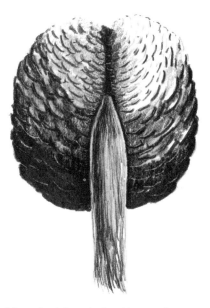

A beard with a circle of breast feathers may be displayed alone, or with wings, tail, and even legs.

A dried beard, with the excess skin trimmed off, can be displayed with a tail mount by gluing or fastening it to the same surface the tail mount is on. If you prefer, the body end of a beard will fit in an empty shell casing of the proper size and can be hung as a novel decoration. Or, instead of a shell casing, you can fashion a soft buckskin cap around the end of the beard and display it that way.

Saving Wings

Wings aren't often saved, although they make a nice display on the wall of your den or lodge. Remove wings at the joint closest to the body. They too will dry. During hot weather it is better to either remove as much flesh as possible, treat with borax or salt to dry, or put in the freezer until you have time to work on them.

Wings are easily removed at the joint closest to the body.

Wings can be displayed spread out, as if in flight, or folded; the latter is the desired position if you're nailing wings when still fresh. In either position they make a good wall decoration for den or lodge.

Saving Spurs and Legs

Remove legs at the joint above the spurs. They can be dried, but the toes must be spread and held in position or they will curl as they dry.

Usually it is only the spurs that are saved as a trophy. With a meat saw, other fine-toothed saw, or hacksaw, cut the leg off above and below the spur. Peel the scaly leg covering off. Remove the section of tendon that runs parallel to the leg and push the marrow out of the bone with a piece of insulated electrical wire.

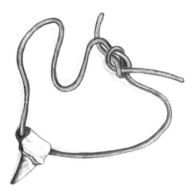

Individual spurs may be displayed in many ways: strung on rawhide, on a hat band, or as a belt decoration.

The spur and bone can then be boiled, or scraped and put in hydrogen peroxide, to whiten.

The spur on its section of leg, left plain or colored, can then be strung on a thong to dry and to display.

If you wish to preserve a leg to show the tremendous size of the foot, use your ingenuity. One way is to pierce the bottom of the foot with a sharp knife, then drill a hole up through the bottom of the foot into the tendon canal and pass a stiff wire up to hold it straight. The wire coming out of the foot is brought down through a board and fastened. The toes should be

A leg must be held in place until it dries. The staples and wire are then removed, but the nail is left in place.

spread in a normal position, temporarily fastened with small staples, and left to dry. The top of the leg should be trimmed neatly, and salt or borax used to help it dry.

Saving a Tail for Mounting

To save a tail you must dry pluck. The most common mistake is to pluck too far toward the tail and remove the beautiful bronze-barred back feathers. When I know I'm going to save a tail, I start in the middle of the back and actually skin down to the tail and then cut the tail off. If you don't have time to work on mounting the tail within a day or so, wrap it in a brown paper bag and freeze it.

Preserving a Tail by Drying

After removing the tail from the carcass as described above, trim as much flesh as possible from the underside.

Where you're going to display your tail mount will determine how much spread you want. Full spread is nice for an inside display, whereas for a door ornament the thirty-inch width is too much.

With the underside facing you, spread the tail as much as you wish for the final position and nail it to a piece of plywood or on an inside wall of an open shed. Rub the exposed-flesh side with salt or borax. Borax needs to be reapplied every three or four days. Salt is easier to apply and needs to be done only every other week or so. When humidity is high the salt becomes runny and will drip moisture. Mounts made with salt are apt to do this even after they appear to be fully cured. Cover your curing mount with screening to protect it from birds and mice.

Depending on season, humidity, and how well you have removed excess flesh and fat, your mount should be ready to display in three to six months. Trim ragged edges and fasten it, feather-side out, to a small piece of plywood. You can then hang the display on a door with a ribbon or Indian corn. A full-spread display can be placed on an inside wall of a den or lodge with beard, wings, spurs, and/or legs.

Full spreads can be put in a frame or display case with or without the beard, spurs, or other parts. For an inside display, keep careful watch for small maggotlike worms and even clothes moths. A light spraying with moth spray or insecticide may be indicated from time to time.

How to Make a Permanent Tail Mount

If you want a truly permanent mount, one that is insect- and rot-resistant, you must either take the tail to a professional taxidermist or take a bit more time and do it yourself.

If you can't devote several periods of three or four hours of uninterrupted time to making a mount, wrap the fresh tail — removed from the carcass as described earlier — in a brown paper bag and freeze it until you do have time.

To mount your trophy you will need the following:

- Small (16-ounce or less) can of liquid fiberglass body filler, found in auto-supply, craft, or hardware stores
- Piece of foam board, at least 20 x 30 inches
- 20 or more pins or pushpins
- Nail polish remover
- Hot-glue gun and glue
- Pair of scissors
- Sharp knife

1. Trim as much flesh, fat, and soft tissue from the underside of the tail as possible.
2. Before starting to remove feathers, note the way they overlap each other. Remove the feathers in layers, starting with the eighteen large fan feathers. You probably will not be able to pull these without breaking them, so cut between each feather and more or less dissect them out. As you remove the individual feathers place them in order,

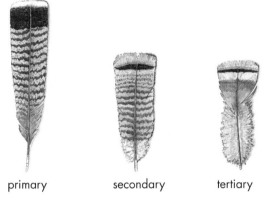

primary   secondary   tertiary

noting that the outside ones are narrow toward the outside of the quill and wide inside the quill.

3. With your knife, scrape each quill until all soft tissue is removed, then wipe with a paper towel to remove fat. Do only one quill at a time and replace them in correct order, topside up.

4. Now remove the second row of feathers. You may be able to pull these one at a time. Again, place each in its proper position, then one at a time scrape, if need be, and wipe each quill with a paper towel.

5. Place the eighteen large fan feathers in correct order and lap position, topside up, on the foam board. Hold them in position with pins. Keep repositioning until you are sure they are the way you want them, usually in a full half circle.

6. Using a brush, cover the quills with a layer of fiberglass, following the dilution directions on the container. Try to encase each quill. After the first layer of material is on, leave it until it hardens. Remove the pins when the fiberglass has set.

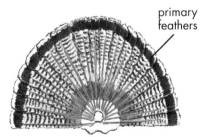

primary
feathers

Using pins to hold the feathers in place, position them as they were on the turkey. Coat the pointed ends with fiberglass resin.

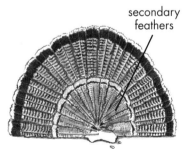

secondary
feathers

When the second coat of resin is firm, remove the pins from the primary feathers. Pin the secondary feathers and coat the quills with resin.

Once the first layer of fiberglass is firm — and depending on the material used, this might be from a few minutes up to two hours — apply a second layer in the same manner, being sure to encase parts of quills not done completely with the first application. Keep the pins in place until fiberglass has set.

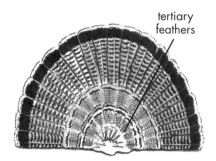

tertiary feathers

Remove the pins from the secondary tail feathers when the resin is set. Shorten and fasten the tertiary feathers either at staggered heights, as they are in nature, or in rows to accentuate the bronze stripe. Use a glue gun.

7. With the second application firm, pin the second row of feathers; be sure they are in the same arc as the fan. When they are placed as you wish, apply a layer of fiberglass to hold them. When the fiberglass has hardened, remove the pins.

8. Cut the third and fourth set of feathers from the skin with scissors, at a level just above the downy section of quill. These are the beautiful bronze-barred feathers. Note their positioning — not in a row forming an arc, like the fan and secondary feathers, but staggered. You may wish to change nature a bit and place them in three separate rows instead of staggering them.

Position them before gluing to see how they fit. When the fiberglass holding the second row is firm, put a dab of hot glue on one feather at a time and attach to the secondary feathers.

9. The next day, when the fiberglass is well cured, slide a wood chisel between the fiberglass mass and the foam board, trying to loosen it. You may have to destroy the foam board to do so, and eventually peel the remains of the foam board coating off the fiberglass.

SAFETY TIP

Observe all the safety precautions on the label of the fiberglass container. For the material to work properly and safely, your workplace should be warm, well ventilated, and away from open flame.

If you get material on your hands or work area, use nail polish remover for cleanup.

I suggest that you try this method on just an ordinary trophy to perfect your technique. Then when you bring home the "big one," you will be able to do it justice.

The finished fan may be placed in a picture frame to display. Or you can hang it by gluing a loop of nylon cord to the back of the fiberglass mass.

Using the fiberglass system of mounting a tail will give you a trophy you can hang anywhere in your home, office, or lodge, with no worms or dirt dropping out. Being able to preserve a beautiful fan from a bird you shot and display it to family, friends, and clients will also preserve your memories. I hope you will try it.

TRIVIA TEST

A good trivia test of how knowledgeable a wild turkey hunter is is to hand him or her a spur and ask if it is right or left. A spur points slightly up on the end and is a bit to the inside of the leg. The groove from the tendon is on the outer side of the bone.

In looking at the reverse side of the finished tail mount,
note the varied location of the quills, outer tail to center.
The feathers must be placed in correct order.

Photography for the Hunter and Nonhunter

A National Wild Turkey Federation emblem in the lower left corner of the rear window of a pickup caught my eye as it pulled up to the diner just ahead of me. The driver, a young man in a green-and-black wool shirt, blue jeans, and Wellington work boots, was out and into the diner before I climbed stiffly out of my car after a hundred-mile drive.

A MAN FOR ALL SEASONS was in prominent letters on the pickup door; above in smaller print was BART SMITH, and underneath, ESTATE CARE. On the bottom was a phone number.

With the breakfast crowd having left and the midmorning coffee and blueberry muffin patrons not yet arrived, the booths were empty in the diner and only a few people sat at the counter. The pickup driver had already been served coffee and was eating a huge blueberry muffin, which meant he was no doubt a local. I sat two stools away and ordered my coffee and muffin.

The man for all seasons smiled and said, "Guess you've been here before. You ordered before looking at the menu."

"Used to come through here a lot, would leave home an hour early so I could be here in time for a big blueberry muffin and still get to Montpelier or UVM in time for a meeting," I replied. Then I said, "I noticed the Wild Turkey Federation sticker on your truck. Are you a turkey hunter?"

Again he smiled, and said, "Oh, yes. I guess everyone is. Now that we have a fall season for turkeys, I notice more people here during quiet season, the time between fall foliage and deer hunting."

"What do you hunt with?"

Now, very serious, the Vermonter teasing the out-of-stater, "A short XI Fast Flight Bow, a 12-gauge Ithaca Turkeyslayer, but mostly my Olympus Zoom 2000 and my JVC compact VHS."

"Do you get many?" I asked.

"Oh, yes. I often get my limit with the bow and shotgun. With the cameras I can hunt all year, and shoot some real beauties. Would you like to see some?" Sliding off the stool, not waiting for an answer, he continued, "I just happen to have some in the truck."

As I admired some of the best wild turkey photos I'd ever seen he told me his story. Returning to the family dairy farm after a hitch in the Marines and four years of college with a degree in landscape design, he found it not big enough to support two families.

Many of the small farms were now weekend estates, and the owners needed caretakers year-round. He started with a few and soon had all the clients he could handle, doing everything from landscape design to lawn mowing and snow plowing. In late spring, summer, and early fall he had to hire help, available from the people who worked at the ski areas in winter. In fall and during spring turkey season he was busy but still had time to hunt. In winter he could handle the work alone and have time to ski and snowshoe.

Many of the estates he serviced would not permit hunting and wanted him to patrol. He started carrying a camera and then a camcorder to take pictures of the wildlife, particularly the increasing number of wild turkeys.

Not restricted to gunning and bow seasons, he could take photographs or video footage any time of year. Another plus was that, since he didn't deal with heavily hunted gun-shy birds, he could capture some wonderful still and video scenes.

The man for all seasons was a lucky man; his profession and his hobbies blended into one, and he was happy.

There are more publications with information on photography than on wild turkeys. In this chapter I'll discuss photography of wild turkeys — without attempting to delve into the intricate detail of the art and science of photography that those publications furnish. I'll talk about the things that I believe the average wild turkey hunter or watcher should know to take good photos or videos and enjoy doing so.

Equipment

You do not have to be a camera buff or a serious photographer and you do not need to go out and buy the most sophisticated equipment to take wonderful pictures of wild turkeys. With all the high-tech, simple-to-use, economically priced photo and video equipment available today, you have a wide selection to choose from.

- Select equipment that is simple to operate, reasonably priced, and will focus automatically.
- Equipment should be small, unobtrusive, and quiet. Once you find what appears to be a small-enough camera or camcorder, try several brands and models in the store to check the noise level.
- Some authorities recommend using a tripod or stand so that results will not be "shaky." Yet some of the best still and video footage I've seen was taken by hand. The more cumbersome your equipment, the more chance there is for sound or glare to frighten your subject.
- As far as film and camcorder tape are concerned, buy the best available, and lots of them so you can keep shooting and not worry about saving for a better shot. Some of what doesn't appear worthwhile through the lens may turn out to be your best work. You can always edit and throw out the poor stuff, but you can't run back to the store to get more film when the shot of a lifetime catches you with an empty camera or camcorder.
- Buy the most sensitive film and tape available. The most interesting actions of spring wild turkeys, those that you would like to put on film or tape, occur prior to full light in the morning.
- Always have an extra battery for your camcorder with you when shooting. A device to run your camcorder from the twelve-volt system in your car can save the camcorder battery, and perhaps the day, when you are shooting from the car.
- To take pictures of wild turkeys, you and your equipment have to be camouflaged, or at least not readily noticed by your subject. You may consider such aids as portable blinds and a flock of decoys to be unnecessary for turkey hunting. For video or photo work, however, they are almost a must.
- Share your work with other photographers and videographers; ask to see theirs. Learn what works for them and try it in your own setting. Besides trial and error, other people's experiences are the best tools to learn from.

Technique

In the early days of wild turkey hunting and of camcorders two hunter friends of mine set up a camcorder on a tripod with a switch they could operate from a blind. They got footage of their calling and the sound of a gobbler answering, then switched off the camcorder. When the gobbler finally came in close enough that they felt he could be seen by the camcorder, they turned it on again. The second the whirring of the camcorder started, the tom took off.

They had tried and, as in all experiences of turkey hunting, they learned. Today they have a collection of "bloopers, blunders, and wonders," as they refer to it, full of memories, laughs, and cheers, all of which they should be proud of.

To secure worthwhile photos or tapes of wild turkey hunting, or just of wild turkeys in their natural habitat, you must combine all your turkey hunting knowledge with all your imagination and ingenuity.

Nonhunting photos and tapes are most easily secured before hunting season or in areas that are restricted to hunting. Landowners who won't allow hunting will sometimes, with a little diplomacy on your part, let you come in to take pictures. Just as a landowner who allows you to hunt appreciates the gift, or at least the offer of a gift, of a nicely dressed turkey, a landowner who allows you to photograph might appreciate copies of some of your results.

Hunting Videos

There seems to be a glut of hunting videos listed for sale in most publications dealing with wild turkeys. A few are undoubtedly excellent but all too often they seem "genuine phony" — too easy, too perfect, with results too predictable. Even for teaching purposes, it's sort of like your six-year-old watching a World Cup ski race to learn how to ski.

I see no reason why two or three ordinary turkey hunters who know how to work together, with a little imagination, ingenuity, modern photo equipment, and aids such as blinds and decoys, couldn't make a realistic turkey hunting video. Sure, there will be mistakes and — as in real life — rarely a sequence ending with a dead trophy bird. But friends would enjoy it because it would be real. A novice could watch it and realize that if everything went like the professional tapes, it wouldn't be that much fun. Best of all, the hunters will have something to add to the pleasure of their memories.

In taking videotapes don't just show hunters, cover, and turkeys. In the beginning, during the waiting periods, and again at the end, pan the background scenery, mountains, hills, and open spaces. The views that surround us when we hunt are never seen by those who don't. They should be part of the record too.

Nonhunting Shots

If you are fortunate enough, as I am, to live in an area inhabited by turkeys, deer, and other wildlife, year-round opportunities for photos and video footage present themselves. Whether you are in your vehicle, out for a walk, or eating a meal, equipment must always be available and ready for the strutting tom or the hen and her brood wandering across your field of view. Here I should say, "Do as I suggest, not as I do." For me, all too often the camcorder battery is low or the camera with the zoom lens is empty, with no film available.

Of course, you can go out shooting pictures with your photo equipment just as the hunter goes out with a bow or shotgun. Using hunting techniques, camouflage, blinds, calls, and decoys will certainly increase your chances of shots, although they will not be as natural as those that just suddenly appear while walking or driving around.

Don't Be Afraid to Experiment

Just as in hunting wild turkeys, the more you work at photographing and videotaping them, the more skill and enjoyment you will gain. Don't be afraid to experiment and develop new techniques of your own. If you combine photographing, hunting, and preserving trophies, you will have a store of memories both for yourself and to share.

For further discussion of photos, particularly taking pictures of recently killed birds, please refer to page 113.

Recipes

COLLECTED AND WRITTEN BY ELINOR METTLER

Serving a wild turkey that you have brought home from the woods or fields, rather than the usual brand-name turkey from the supermarket, surely lends a special flavor to your Thanksgiving or Christmas dinner. How special it is to provide for your family feast in this way. When the children in the family read before about the first Thanksgiving or an old-fashioned Christmas on the farm, it was just a story. Now it's as though they were living in those more picturesque times, and a new family tradition begins.

Earlier chapters explained how the wild turkey differs from the domestic bird. Roaming, running, and flying in the wild, the wild bird is naturally leaner than one grown in a pen and bred for plumpness. But it can be prepared according to any recipe for domestic turkey.

The current interest in eating lower-fat foods and avoiding cholesterol has increased the popularity of turkey — not just the usual roast turkey, popular for special occasions or buffets, but also various other forms, such as turkey cutlets and ground turkey.

The following recipes have been collected from many good cooks — friends, family, and professional chefs. Each cook adds a personal touch to a recipe, and of course you may do the same!

There are many ways in which the meat of your wild turkey can be cooked and served. But let's begin with various recipes for the golden brown bird brought to the feasting table — the old favorite, roast turkey.

TRADITIONAL ROAST TURKEY

Although a few alternative methods follow, this is the way most people like to prepare and roast their wild turkey.

1. Pluck any remaining pinfeathers from bird. Rinse and dry cavity. Fill with your choice of stuffing, and place on a rack in a roasting pan.
2. Lay 3 or 4 slices of bacon over breast and cover loosely with foil. Also wrap each leg in foil to prevent its drying during roasting.
3. With oven at 350°F, roast a small unstuffed turkey (up to 10 pounds) 3 to 4 hours, a 10- to 16-pound bird 3½ to 4½ hours, a large bird 4 to 5 hours, or until a meat thermometer registers 170°F. Add ½ hour in each case for a stuffed turkey. Baste occasionally and remove foil during last ½ hour for browning. Do not overcook.
4. Vary this method by using a basting sauce instead of the bacon. Baste every hour or more frequently as desired.

EDNA'S VARIATION

Edna Dawson discovered what she considers a foolproof method for keeping a wild turkey moist during roasting — plastic roasting bags.

1. Place cut up apple or onion in cavity; bake stuffing separately.
2. Place unstuffed bird within plastic cooking bag.
3. Roast 2 to 2½ hours for a 12 to 16 pound bird, 3 to 3½ hours for a large 20 to 24 pounder.
4. Split bag for the last ½ hour of roasting to increase browning.

CARVING A TURKEY

Remove leg at the joint.   Remove wing at the joint.   Slice from the breast.

THAWING A FROZEN WILD TURKEY

If you're thawing a turkey in the refrigerator, do so in its original wrapping and according to the times below. When thawing turkey in cold water, change the water every 30 minutes.

Weight	Refrigerator	Cold Water
8–12 lbs.	1–2 days	4–6 hrs.
12–16 lbs.	2–3 days	6–9 hrs.
16–20 lbs.	3–4 days	9–11 hrs.
20–24 lbs.	4–5 days	11–12 hrs.

ROAST WILD TURKEY BREAST

David and Irene Silvernail prefer to roast only the turkey breast, using the legs and thighs for soup. This is Irene's method for roasting wild turkey.

1. Sprinkle sage, poultry seasoning, salt, and pepper over breast and top with bacon strips. Place in a roasting pan and cover loosely with foil.
2. Roast at 350 to 375°F, 15 minutes per pound. A half hour before done, remove foil for browning.

FLORA'S ROAST WILD TURKEY BREAST

Flora Bergquist likes to roast only the turkey breast now that the children have grown and she's cooking for just her husband Herb and herself.

1. Place breast on a large sheet of foil, baste with margarine, and season with salt and pepper. Completely enclose meat in foil and seal.
2. Bake at 325°F for 1½ hours for a moist roast. Thicken juice with cornstarch.

AN AMERICAN TRADITION

In rural communities all over America the turkey supper, put on by a church or Grange, is a long-standing tradition. They are most often held in autumn, making them an important stop on the campaign trail for town and county politicians eager to shake the hands of the happily well-fed crowd.

Wild turkey can add a special flavor to such a bounteous supper, along with all the usual fixin's . . . mashed potatoes, mashed turnips, lots of stuffing and gravy, a side of coleslaw, and those soft rolls that are always served at these suppers.

Surely one of the longest-running turkey suppers in the country must be the one put on by the folks at St. John's Lutheran Church in Ancram, New York. It's hard for them to remember how many consecutive years they've been cheerfully preparing their annual supper, but their best guess is around seventy.

With all the cooks involved, they say no two dishes ever turn out quite the same, but for one that topped off the feast. It was made by a woman who taught generations of local schoolchildren and who served on the church council and as Sunday school superintendent until she died at the age of eighty-nine. This is her recipe.

BEULAH BOUCHER'S MINCE PIE

2   packages mincemeat
½   glass currant jelly
    A little sugar, cinnamon, and cloves
    Small piece of apple, cut up
    A few more raisins

Prepare mincemeat according to package directions. Add other ingredients and place in a pie shell. Bake 30 minutes at 425°F.

We'd love your thoughts . . .

Your reactions, criticisms, things you did or didn't like about this Storey Book. Please use space below (or write a letter if you'd prefer — even send photos!) telling how you've made use of the information . . . how you've put it to work . . . the more details the better!

Thanks in advance for your help in building our library of good Storey Books.

Pamela B. Art

Publisher, Storey Books

Book Title: _____

Purchased From: _____

Comments: _____

_____

_____

_____

_____

_____

Your Name: _____

Mailing Address: _____

E-mail Address: _____

☐ Please check here if you'd like our latest Storey's Books for Country Living Catalog, (or call 800-441-5700 to order).

☐ You have my permission to quote from my comments and use these quotations in ads, brochures, mail, and other promotions used to market Storey Books.

Signed _____ Date _____

e-mail=thoughts@storey.com   www.storeybooks.com   * Printed in the USA   03/00

From: _____

BUSINESS REPLY MAIL

FIRST-CLASS MAIL   PERMIT NO. 2   POWNAL VT

POSTAGE WILL BE PAID BY ADDRESSEE

STOREY'S BOOKS FOR COUNTRY LIVING
STOREY COMMUNICATIONS INC
RR1 BOX 105
POWNAL VT 05261-9988

KIT'S EGGPLANT STUFFING

*Kit Sigety, who roasts turkeys on a farm in Pipersville, Pennsylvania,
places the stuffing under the skin to keep the breast meat moist,
a method she learned from her Hungarian mother-in-law.*

4 medium onions, chopped coarse	½ cup chopped parsley
6 stalks celery, chopped	Salt, pepper, and poultry seasoning
2 tablespoons butter or margarine	1 quart bread cubes
1 eggplant, peeled and diced	lemon, cut in half

1. Sauté onions and celery in butter. Add eggplant and parsley, and sauté a bit more. Add seasonings and toss in bread cubes. Moisten with water if mixture seems dry.
2. Gently raise skin off meat, starting at rear of breast. Skin will stretch as you raise it over breast to wings and legs. Rub lemon on meat and cover with a layer of stuffing. Gently replace skin.
3. Fill cavity in usual way, keeping stuffing light, not packed.

SWEET POTATO STUFFING

Veterinarian Jeanne Logue likes to refrigerate her stuffing overnight to blend flavors.

1¼ cups mashed sweet potato	1¼ teaspoons salt
4 cups toasted bread cubes (or croutons)	¼ teaspoon black pepper
½ cup finely chopped celery	¼ teaspoon sage
⅓ cup chopped fresh onion	¼ teaspoon crumbled whole marjoram leaves
6 link sausages, cut into ½-inch pieces	½ teaspoon ground thyme
	2 tablespoons butter

1. Combine first 4 ingredients in mixing bowl.
2. Brown sausage and add to mixture, discarding fat.
3. Blend in remaining ingredients. Mix and spoon into turkey cavity.
4. Cook turkey immediately after stuffing.

EVELYN'S STUFFING

Our daughter Sally doesn't have a lot of time for cooking. But tradition is important to her, and when the holidays come she goes all out. She learned this recipe while a music therapist at a mental health center. "Every year the staff cooked at least eight turkeys and many side dishes to serve clients a Thanksgiving dinner. When John, our janitor, arrived with his turkey we surrounded him to sample his wife, Evelyn's, stuffing. Finally, she shared her recipe with us."

1	pound Italian sausages	2	apples, chopped
1	stalk celery, chopped	1	cup applesauce
1	green pepper, chopped	½	cup raisins
1	medium onion, chopped	¼	cup melted butter
2	cloves garlic, minced	2	ounces apricot brandy
1	loaf toasting bread, or unsliced stuffing bread (or large bag of stuffing mix)		Salt, pepper, Bell's, and Italian seasonings to taste Chicken or turkey stock

1. Remove casings from sausage; place in skillet over medium-low heat. Crumble with fork and cook slowly for about 5 minutes. Add chopped celery, pepper, and onion, plus garlic. Continue cooking, stirring mixture, until wilted.
2. Break bread into pieces and place in a bowl. Mix in sausage mixture. Add apples, applesauce, raisins, butter, brandy, and seasonings, and moisten with chicken or turkey stock. Stuff bird lightly.

VARIATIONS ON EVELYN'S STUFFING

Add 1 cup sliced cranberries or dates before stuffing bird. Also, experiment with other fruit-flavored brandies.

GRANDMA'S SAUSAGE STUFFING

Our daughter Jody has always made her grandmother's sausage stuffing for turkey, and now she's making it for the wild turkey brought home by her son Joe. No matter whether she's at her own home for a holiday or back home with us, it's Jody who makes the stuffing.

1	pound bulk sausage
½	cup chopped onion
2	loaves unsliced stuffing bread
1	cup chopped celery
1	tablespoon Bell's seasoning
1	teaspoon pepper
2	eggs

1. Break up bulk sausage into a skillet and cook over medium heat until thoroughly cooked. Push to one side and sauté chopped onion.

2. Break stuffing bread into a large bowl. Add chopped celery and the onion and sausage, including drippings in skillet. Add Bell's poultry seasoning, pepper, and eggs. If necessary, add a bit of water to bind ingredients.

3. Stuff neck and body cavities lightly. Bake extra stuffing in a greased bowl, placing it in oven about 45 minutes before turkey is ready.

SAFETY TIP

Never place stuffing in a turkey until ready to roast. Until then, keep it refrigerated in a separate bowl. This impedes bacterial growth and prevents food poisoning.

BEST BARBECUE SAUCE

If barbecuing is your favorite method of cooking, a small young turkey, about 6 pounds, can be cut into pieces and cooked on the grill as you would chicken. Try the Mettler family's "Best" for a succulent result.

⅔	cup butter or margarine	2	tablespoons pickle, chopped (optional)
2	tablespoons sugar		
1	teaspoon salt	2	teaspoons Worcestershire sauce
	Few grains cayenne	1½	tablespoons lemon juice
2	tablespoons flour	¼	cup vinegar
⅔	cup water or stock	¼	teaspoon Tabasco sauce

1. Melt butter or margarine in small saucepan. Combine dry ingredients and add to pan, stirring until well blended. Remove from heat. Combine remaining ingredients and gradually stir into butter mixture. Return to heat and cook, stirring constantly, until thick and smooth. Refrigerate until ready to use; this will thicken sauce further, making it easier to brush on meat.
2. Grill turkey over hot coals to sear each side, then brush on sauce, continuing as pieces are turned, for about 45 minutes on lowered heat.

DEEP-FRYING SOUTHERN-STYLE

The most unusual way to cook a whole wild turkey is to deep-fry it Southern-style with Cajun seasoning.

Rather than marinating the bird in the seasoning for hours, it can be injected with the sauce just a few minutes prior to cooking. The Chef Williams Cajun Injector is one on the market that gives directions on points where the bird should be injected.

This type of cooking should be done outdoors on the gas grill, and done with great care. A frozen turkey must be thoroughly thawed and the bird totally dry, inside and out, before immersing it in hot oil, to prevent spattering. It is not to be stuffed.

In order to remove the cooked bird from the oil, cotton string can be tied securely around it with loops hanging over the sides of the pot to lift it or a wire coat hanger can be hooked to a band holding the drumsticks together.

Turkey Call: The Magazine of the Wild Turkey Federation gives hints on deep-frying, including how to determine the amount of peanut oil you need for the cooking: Fill a deep cooking vessel with water and lower the turkey into it; the water should just cover the bird but not spill over. Remove the turkey and measure the amount of water. Discard the water and replace it with the same amount of oil (probably 3 to 5 gallons). Again, dry the bird thoroughly before placing it in the oil, which should be at 350°F for cooking.

Sources of information on deep-frying suggest 3 1/2 to 4 1/2 minutes per pound. The turkey will rise to the top of the oil when cooked.

When done, allow the turkey to sit awhile before carving.

KEVIN'S GRILLED TURKEY CUTLETS

Kevin Silvernail is not only the hunter providing the wild turkey, but also the chef presiding over his outdoor grill or smoker.

1. Slice breast into cutlets and pound. Marinate in orange juice or apple cider (Kevin makes the latter in his press). Or make a marinade of equal parts vinegar and oil, plus poultry seasoning, salt, and pepper. Simmer marinade ½ hour and let cool. Soak cutlets overnight.
2. Cook cutlets 20 minutes on gas grill or over charcoal (with wood for a smoky flavor), basting with marinade.

TURKEY PARMESAN

There are many ways to enjoy your turkey by dividing it into parts. For example, there is a wide variety of recipes for cutlets cut from the breast. Some of these provide quick, easy, and delicious meals, such as this favorite of Jody's family, which can easily be doubled.

    4   turkey cutlets
    2   tablespoons butter or margarine
    ½   cup mayonnaise
    ¼   cup Parmesan cheese

1. Sauté turkey cutlets in butter or margarine, or bake on buttered baking sheet in 400°F oven, until no longer pink.
2. Meanwhile, mix mayonnaise and grated Parmesan cheese. Spread mixture on cutlets and place under broiler for a few minutes until brown and bubbly.

WIENER SCHNITZEL

One of our family's favorites is Wiener schnitzel, which can be made with turkey breast. Our daughter Meg is a gourmet cook, and this is her recipe.

1¼	pounds turkey cutlets, pounded thin	2½	cups fresh bread crumbs
1½	cups flour	2	tablespoons cooking oil
2	eggs plus 2 tablespoons water, lightly beaten	6	tablespoons butter
		1	fresh lemon
		¼	cup capers

1. Dip meat in flour, then egg, then bread crumbs, patting to coat well. Place in no more than 2 layers on plate, cover with waxed paper, and refrigerate at least ½ hour.
2. Heat oil in a skillet. Cook cutlets quickly over medium-high heat until coating is browned.
3. Serve with melted butter, lemon wedges, and capers.

SAVORY TURKEY PIE

A deep dish pie is an easy way to use cooked turkey for a delicious supper. Add cooked vegetables if you wish to make it a one dish meal.

4	tablespoons margarine	2	cups (or more) cut-up cooked turkey
⅓	cup flour		
¼	teaspoon salt	2½	cups (approximate) biscuit dough
⅛	teaspoon pepper		
1⅓	cups turkey broth	¼	teaspoon paprika
⅔	cup milk	¼	teaspoon celery salt

1. Melt margarine in a saucepan. Add flour, salt, and pepper. Stir in turkey broth and milk. Cook until thickened, and then add 2 cups or more of cut-up cooked turkey.
2. Pour into baking dish.
3. Top with 1 recipe of biscuit dough (Bisquick is good) to which you have added paprika and celery salt.
4. Bake at 425°F 25 minutes or until nicely browned.

PLAINVILLE TURKEY BREAST MARSALA

*At Plainville Turkey Farm in New York's Finger Lakes district,
the William Ward family produces more than 450,000 turkeys a year.
The farm has become famous for its turkey products and busy restaurant,
where diners can enjoy the following three original recipes.*

1	beaten egg	1	pound turkey breast
¼	cup milk		cutlets ½" thick, pounded
1	cup Italian bread	¼	cup butter
	crumbs	2	tablespoons oil
½	cup Parmesan cheese	¼	cup marsala wine
2	teaspoons poultry	1	cup sliced fresh mushrooms,
	seasoning		sautéed

1. Combine egg and milk in a shallow dish. On a flat plate combine crumbs, cheese, and seasoning. Dip turkey in egg mixture, then crumbs, coating thickly.
2. In a skillet melt 1 tablespoon butter with 1 tablespoon oil. Sauté a few slices of turkey at a time over low heat for 5 minutes, adding more oil and butter as needed.
3. When all slices are cooked, return them to skillet, add wine, cover, and simmer for 2 minutes. Serve immediately, topped with mushrooms.

MARINATED PLAINVILLE TURKEY THIGHS

½	cup vinegar	1	garlic clove, smashed
⅛	cup lemon juice	½	teaspoon pepper
½	cup oil	2	turkey thighs
2	tablespoons oregano		

1. Combine first 6 ingredients and pour over thighs arranged in a glass dish. Cover and refrigerate overnight, turning thighs occasionally.
2. Preheat oven to 350°F. Remove turkey from marinade and arrange in shallow baking dish, skin-side down. Bake 30 minutes. Turn skin-side up, baste with marinade, and continue baking, basting often, until temperature of meat reaches 185°F.

PLAINVILLE TURKEY STIR-FRY

3	tablespoons teriyaki sauce	12	ounces mushrooms, sliced
3	tablespoons cooking sherry	1	medium onion, sliced
¼	teaspoon garlic powder	1	green pepper, sliced
3	tablespoons cornstarch	3	small summer squash, sliced
4	turkey cutlets, sliced	10	ounces snow peas
¼	cup oil	10	cherry tomatoes, halved

1. Mix teriyaki, sherry, garlic powder, and cornstarch; pour over meat and cover.
2. Pour 2 tablespoons oil into a skillet or wok; add mushrooms, onion, pepper, and squash, and stir-fry 4 minutes. Remove from pan.
3. Add remaining oil; heat to high and stir-fry turkey mixture 4 minutes.
4. Add snow peas, cooked vegetables, and tomatoes. Cook until warm.

TURKEY TETRAZZINI

This family favorite makes good use of leftover turkey.

8 SERVINGS

1	8-ounce package medium wide noodles	2	cups turkey stock
		1	cup heavy cream
6	tablespoons butter or margarine	⅓	cup sherry
		1	6-ounce can mushrooms
6	tablespoons flour	⅓	cup slivered almonds
1½	teaspoons salt	3	teaspoons minced parsley
¼	teaspoon pepper	2	cups diced turkey
½	teaspoon celery salt	½	cup Parmesan cheese

1. Cook noodles until tender and drain.
2. Melt butter, add flour, and blend. Add seasonings and stock (or use 2 cups turkey gravy); cook over low heat until thick, stirring constantly.
3. Remove from heat, stir in cream (scalded), sherry, mushrooms, almonds, and parsley.
4. Alternate layers of noodles, turkey, and sauce in 2-quart greased casserole. Top with cheese. Bake at 350°F for 45 minutes.

OLD FAVORITE CHILI

Ground turkey has become a popular substitute for hamburger, particularly with those who avoid red meat. The next three recipes call for cut up and ground wild turkey meat, which you can prepare yourself.

2	tablespoons oil	2½	cups canned tomatoes, cut up with juices (1 large can)
1	medium onion, chopped		
1	green pepper, chopped	2½	cups canned kidney beans, undrained (2 medium cans)
1	red pepper, chopped (optional)		
		2	teaspoons salt
1	pound ground turkey (dark meat)	1	teaspoon chili powder

1. Heat oil in a heavy kettle over low heat; add onion and peppers and sauté about 3 minutes until soft and slightly browned. Add remaining ingredients, browning meat lightly.
2. Cover and place in 300°F oven for 2 hours.

CRANBERRY TURKEY BURGER

At the St. Charles Hotel, a landmark in the riverside city of Hudson, New York, the chef has two turkey sandwiches on the lunch menu, including the burger below.

1	pound fresh ground turkey		Salt and pepper to taste
		½	cup cranberry sauce
1	teaspoon rubbed sage	½	cup mayonnaise

1. Thoroughly mix ground turkey with sage, salt, and pepper. Make 4 patties. Grill or broil until well done (165°F in center, approximately 5 minutes on each side).
2. Remove burgers to skillet that has half the cranberry sauce in it. Glaze burgers for about a minute on each side.
3. Mix remaining cranberry sauce and mayonnaise to form dressing. Place burger on a fresh roll and garnish with lettuce, tomato, and a dab of dressing.

TURKEY ENCHILADAS

Our daughter Suzanne and her husband, Wayne, are both professors, each busy with teaching and research. But at home they cook together, and this Mexican dish is a favorite for entertaining.

SAUCE

2 teaspoons oil
2 cloves garlic, minced
⅔ cup onion, chopped fine
⅓ cup green pepper, chopped fine
1 small can minced green chilies
1 large can tomatoes, chopped, with juices
¼ teaspoon cumin
¼ teaspoon salt
¼ teaspoon fresh ground pepper

ENCHILADAS

2 teaspoons oil
1 large clove garlic, minced
1 pound ground turkey
1 tablespoon chili powder
1 16-ounce can black beans, undrained
16 (approximately) corn tortillas
1 cup Monterey jack cheese, shredded

1. FOR SAUCE: Heat oil in a large skillet; add garlic, onion, pepper, and chilies, and sauté 5 to 7 minutes. Add remaining sauce ingredients.
2. Bring sauce to boil over medium heat, lower heat, and simmer 15 minutes, stirring occasionally. Set aside.
3. FOR ENCHILADAS: Heat oil in a large skillet; add garlic and sauté 30 seconds. Add turkey and chili powder and sauté, breaking up turkey until all browned. Stir in beans with liquid.
4. Heat oven to 350°F. Soften tortillas one at a time in a bit of oil (do not brown). Place ¼ cup turkey-bean mixture on each tortilla and roll it closed; set enchiladas seam down in greased 13x9x2 inch pan. Cover with sauce, then cheese. Bake 25 minutes.

GOOD-BYE TURKEY SOUP

When Irene Silvernail roasts only the breast of David's turkey (see page 135), she doesn't discard all the rest. She makes a hearty stock using the legs and thighs as the base, then adds celery, onions, carrots, thyme, bay leaf, parsley, and rice or orzo.

Like most experienced cooks, she doesn't measure when cooking something like a homemade soup and uses pretty much whatever is at hand. In this case she might even add leftover vegetables, because nothing goes to waste in a good cook's kitchen. And this simmers on the back burner of her woodstove until its wonderful aroma brings Dave in to supper.

The Silvernail family is all grown up now, so Irene no longer cooks for a family of six, but our daughter Jody does. And after all the turkey that can be cut from the bone has been eaten, she cooks the carcass for a postholiday soup.

1. Cook carcass 2 to 3 hours in water to cover (about 6 quarts) for a good broth. Remove from pot, pick off remaining meat, and reserve. Refrigerate broth overnight and skim off any fat accumulated on top (little or none from the lean wild turkey).
2. Chop an onion and a few stalks of celery and cook in a little broth, then add to pot. Add 1/2 to 3/4 cup rice (about a handful). Simmer about 15 minutes. Return meat to broth and add a 20-ounce bag of frozen mixed vegetables, plus salt and pepper to taste. Cook 10 minutes.

While visiting Jody in Maryland, we had lunch at the Meadow Lark Inn in rural Poolesville, where they gave their turkey soup a creole twist by adding tomatoes and green pepper.

The Next Generation

Look, Grandpa, tracks!" six-year-old Chris whispered excitedly. "They must have been here since the rain."

Before our evening walk down Maple Lane, my wife and I had promised our visiting grandchildren that they would see deer and, if we were lucky, wild turkeys, and all sorts of smaller creatures. The promise was made with a disclaimer: "If you all will be very quiet."

Chris had been very quiet, going along as though he was playing "going on a lion hunt." The rest of the group, with all that had to be said to each other after not being together for six months, made enough noise to clear the alfalfa fields and hedgerows on either side of this dead-end lane of all visible wildlife.

To sharp-eyed Chris, though, there were things that the rest did not see. He hung back to examine the deer tracks in the soft dirt at the edge of the gravel road, and then caught my eye with a hand motion. Suddenly everyone was quiet, watching where Chris was pointing to an ancient chestnut fence post. Most noticeable was a small black shining eye. Slowly, almost imperceptibly, the reddish brown head of a chipmunk appeared out of the top of the post.

Like a reverse jack-in-the-box the head would in a flash disappear, and then very slowly reappear to stare at this strange group of creatures staring in silent awe at him.

On succeeding evenings the group, with Chris leading, was quiet. They were rewarded with the sight of deer in their summer red, rabbits,

149

squirrels, and, one evening, a maple tree full of roosting turkeys. They had great fun at dusk drawing curious deer in close by snapping a white handkerchief. Still, the most memorable sight was the curious chipmunk.

Will there be wildlife for children to observe through the next century? Will there be wildlife for young men and women to hunt? Will there be young men and women who want to hunt?

I doubt if even the people in the field of human behavior know the answers. But I am convinced that if the answer to the third question is "no," the answer to the first two questions will also be a resounding "no."

The wild turkey is the best example of an almost extinct species brought back through the efforts and funding of those who enjoy hunting. There are probably more people who enjoy watching wild turkeys than those who hunt them. Thus, the second group benefits from the efforts of the first.

WILL THERE BE TOO MANY TURKEYS?

At present, turkey numbers seem to increase each year, pointing out that even with more hunters and better hunting techniques, the turkey is thriving. But how many turkeys is too many for an area? Will loss of habitat cause numbers to dwindle or, as with our local Canada goose and the white-tailed deer, will their numbers increase and become a nuisance?

As a veterinarian, I am aware of the danger of disease from overpopulation. The game commissions and environmental conservation departments in the various states and provinces have done a wonderful job of bringing the wild turkey back from near-extinction. They deserve our support both politically and by observing the regulations they establish. Any variation in hunting methods should be within the scope of these regulations.

To a six-year-old the adventure of seeing the antics of a chipmunk is just as great as watching a curious doe come across a field at dusk to investigate a flashing white handkerchief. The six-year-old soon learns that when the wind is blowing toward the deer, she detects his presence and won't come.

Next he learns to read deer language — that is, to tell by the deer's stance, head, and tail motions whether she is curious, nervous, or alerted and frightened. He learns turkey talk — the danger signal, "puck! puck!"; the signal to come to your mother, "chur chur." He learns that the sandpiper with the broken wing is a mother drawing him away from her young.

Observing, curious youngsters will find the world of wildlife — from frogs to bears and moose, and from hummingbirds to turkey buzzards — more fascinating than television. They will find the real world of rabbits, squirrels, foxes, wild turkeys, deer, and bears to be different from what's portrayed by Disney. As they grow older they will find that their own real world is not all sweetness and light either. But they will also learn that just as the wild turkey and the sandpiper protect their young from the coyote, so they, too, can cope with the threats of life.

Whether youngsters want to participate in hunting as they get close to their teens probably depends as much on environment as heredity. As in any sport, particularly skiing or riding, some are ready at an earlier age than others. And very similarly to those two sports, if a parent tries to push too hard, the child will never enjoy hunting.

Kindergarten teachers and horse trainers know that youngsters have a short attention span. A short walk in fields and woods is fine, but sitting on a deer stand for hours with cold feet can turn a child off not only from hunting but from any participation in observing wildlife as well.

Children take far more notice of bad manners and behavior than most of us realize. When they are with us we must "go by the rules" both in our respect for game regulations and in our observation of gun safety.

Make each trip to the field a teaching and learning experience. Children will notice things that you don't, and ask questions. If you don't know the answers, you should find out. I have a friend, a veterinarian who had degrees in zoology and wildlife management prior to entering veterinary college. A walk in the woods with him is a lesson in itself. If you can't find someone like my friend to answer your children's questions, the National Wild Turkey Federation, with its J.A.K.E.S. program (Juniors Acquiring Knowledge, Ethics, and Sportsmanship) for youngsters, is an excellent source.

Passing on the Tradition

Even if a child never has any possibility of hunting with a gun, boys and girls alike should learn from an early age that guns are not toys. They are made to either hunt and kill animals, or kill other human beings. Children should be taught that even a toy gun should never be pointed at anything — human, animal, or property — that it would not be proper to shoot.

About ten years ago I saw advertised in the Orvis Christmas catalog a miniature double-barrel shotgun made by Edison in Italy. A glorified cap gun, it shoots what look like small shotgun shells with only a primer. It was suggested that it could be used to teach a youngster gun safety. I had seen my grandson Joe playing with friends using everything from sticks to plastic "ray guns" to "kill" each other. With his parents' approval I made him a promise of one of these Orvis Edison training shotguns if he would never even point a stick at another boy making believe it was a gun.

The little shotgun was a beauty, with all the parts of a real gun: safety, breaking latch, separate trigger for each barrel, and even a sling.

After Christmas morning it was locked in the gun cabinet next to my firearms. Joe's first lesson was that the gun was "real," and that he was to handle it as such. When it was removed from the cabinet, his first act was to break it and make sure it was not loaded. The safety was always on except in the actual act of firing.

Outdoors, with no other children around, it was loaded with two shells and fired at a suitable safe target. Of course, nothing except a "pop" came out of the barrel when it was fired. After firing half a dozen shells, it was necessary to remove the spent primers and reload each. This assures that it will not be used just to make noise.

The gun did not go home with Joe, but was kept at my home. The following summer Joe carried the gun with me on woodchuck hunts, and in fall, grouse hunting. It was gratifying to see that he observed all the safety precautions that a person should observe with a real gun.

When Joe reached twelve he took the New York State Hunter Safety Training Course. I sat through parts of the twelve-hour course with him, and was surprised that a lot of what was taught was new to me.

Again with his parents' blessing, I bought Joe a 20-gauge pump. My first thought was to plug it so only one shell could be fired at a time, but after watching Joe at the firing part of the hunter safety training I realized that he was careful enough to load more than one shell while actually hunting. For practice and patterning only one shell is loaded at a time.

When Christopher, Joe's cousin, reached the age where he could be learning from the training gun, he seemed more interested in using a bow. He has fired the training gun and when he is ready and asks for it, I will work with him.

Christopher has been hunting with me and has a good respect for guns. As for his observing, curious nature, tracks still fascinate him. He sees more while we are hunting than most adults. Perhaps he will be more interested in studying and watching wildlife than hunting. I just hope there will be enough for him to see as time goes on.

In the meantime, Joe has completed an impressive science project on the differences between wild and domestic turkeys. He has other interests in life, from listening to 1940s music and learning to play it on his trumpet, to watching and playing baseball. When it was time to go home after his most recent successful turkey and squirrel hunting trip, he appeared thoughtful, then said, "Grandpa, hunting is more fun than baseball."

Appendixes

State Game Commissions

Alabama Dept. of Conservation and
Natural Resources
64 Union Street
Montgomery, AL 36130
205-242-3486

Arizona Game and Fish Dept.
2221 West Greenway Road
Phoenix, AZ 85023
602-942-3000

Arkansas Game and Fish Comm.
2 Natural Resources Drive
Little Rock, AR 72205
501-223-6300

California Dept. of Fish and Game
3211 South Street
Sacramento, CA 95816
916-227-2244

Colorado Div. of Wildlife
6060 Broadway
Denver, CO 80216
303-297-1192

Connecticut Dept. of Environmental
Protection
79 Elm Street
Hartford, CT 06106
203-424-3105

Delaware Div. of Fish and Wildlife
89 Kings Highway, P.O. Box 1401
Dover, DE 19903
302-739-4431

Florida Game and Fresh Water Fish
Comm.
620 South Meridian Street
Tallahassee, FL 32399-1660
904-488-4676

Georgia Game and Fish Comm.
270 Washington Street, S.W.
Atlanta, GA 30334

Hawaii Game and Fish Div.
1151 Punchbowl Street
Honolulu, HI 96813
808-587-0077

Idaho Dept. of Fish and Game
Box 25
Boise, ID 83707

Illinois Dept. of Conservation
P.O. Box 19446
Springfield, IL 62794-9446
217-782-7305

Indiana Div. of Fish and Wildlife
615 State Office Building
Indianapolis, IN 46204

Iowa Conservation Comm.
Wallace State Office Building
Des Moines, IA 50319

Kansas Dept. of Wildlife & Parks
512 S.E. 25th
Pratt, KS 67124
316-672-5911

Kentucky Dept. of Fish and Wildlife
  Resources
#1 Game Farm Road
Frankfort, KY 40601
502-564-3400

Louisiana Dept. of Wildlife and
  Fisheries
Wildlife and Fisheries Building
New Orleans, LA 70130

Maine Inland Fisheries and Wildlife
  Licensing
284 State Street
State House Station 41
Augusta, ME 04333

Maryland Dept. of Natural Resources
Tawes State Office Building
Annapolis, MD 21401
301-974-3195

Massachusetts Div. of Fisheries and
  Wildlife
100 Cambridge Street
Boston, MA 02202
617-727-3151

Michigan Wildlife Div.
Department of Natural Resources
Box 30028
Lansing, MI 48909

Minnesota Dept. of Natural
  Resources
500 Lafayette Road
St. Paul, MN 55155-4040
612-296-6157

Mississippi Game and Fish Comm.
P.O. Box 451
Jackson, MS 39205
601-362-9212

Missouri Dept. of Conservation
P.O. Box 180
Jefferson City, MO 65102-0180
314-751-4115

Montana Dept. of Fish, Wildlife &
  Parks
1420 East 6th Street
Helena, MT 59620
406-444-2535

Nebraska Game and Parks Comm.
P.O. Box 30370
Lincoln, NE 68503-0370
402-471-0641

New Hampshire Fish & Game Dept.
2 Hazen Drive
Concord, NH 03301
603-271-3421

New Jersey Div. of Fish, Game, and
  Wildlife
CN-400
Trenton, NJ 08625

New Mexico Dept. of Game and Fish
Villagra Building
Santa Fe, NM 87503
505-827-7885

New York Fish and Wildlife Div.
50 Wolf Road
Albany, NY 12233-4790
518-457-3521

North Carolina Wildlife Resources
  Comm.
325 North Salisbury Street
Raleigh, NC 27611

North Dakota Game and Fish Dept.
2121 Lovett Avenue
Bismarck, ND 58505

Ohio Division of Wildlife
Fountain Square
Columbus, OH 43224

Oklahoma Dept. of Wildlife
    Conservation
1801 North Lincoln
Oklahoma City, OK 73105
405-521-3855

Oregon Dept. of Fish & Wildlife
P.O. Box 59
Portland, OR 97207
503-229-5400

Pennsylvania Game Comm.
2001 Elmerton Avenue
Harrisburg, PA 17110-9797
717-787-4250

Rhode Island Div. of Fish and
    Wildlife
Group Center
Wakefield, RI 02879

South Carolina Wildlife Resources
    Dept.
P.O. Box 167
Columbia, SC 29202

South Dakota Dept. of Game, Fish
    & Parks
Anderson Building
Pierre, SD 57501

Tennessee Valley Authority
100 Van Morgan Drive
Golden Pond, TN 42211
502-924-5602

Texas Parks & Wildlife Dept.
4200 Smith School Road
Austin, TX 78744
512-389-4800

Utah Div. of Wildlife Resources
1596 West Temple
Salt Lake City, UT 84116

Vermont Fish and Wildlife Dept.
103 South Main
Waterbury, VT 05676
802-244-7331

Virginia Comm. of Game
Box 11104
Richmond, VA 23230-1104
804-367-1000

Washington Dept. of Wildlife
600 Capitol Way North
Olympia, WA 98501-1091
206-753-5700

West Virginia Dept. of Natural
    Resources
1900 Kanawah Boulevard East
Charleston, WV 25305
304-558-2758

Wisconsin Dept. of Natural Resources
P.O. Box 7921
Madison, WI 53707
608-226-1877

Wyoming Game & Fish Dept.
5400 Bishop Boulevard
Cheyenne, WY 82202
307-777-4601

Ontario, Canada
Ontario Natural Resource
    Information Center
MNR, 300 Water Street, Box 700
Peterborough, Ontario, Canada K9J
    8M5
705-755-2000

Wild Turkey Hunting Seasons

State	Seasons	Subspecies
Alabama	Spring/Fall	Eastern
Arizona	Spring/Fall	Merriam's
Arkansas	Spring/Fall	Eastern
California	Spring/Fall	Rio Grande, Merriam's
Colorado	Spring/Fall	Merriam's
Connecicut	Spring/Fall	Eastern
Delaware	Spring	Eastern
Florida	Spring/Fall	Eastern, Osceola
Georgia	Spring	Eastern
Hawaii	Spring/Fall	Rio Grande
Idaho	Spring	Merriam's
Illinois	Spring/Fall	Eastern
Indiana	Spring	Eastern
Iowa	Spring/Fall	Eastern
Kansas	Spring/Fall	Rio Grande, Eastern
Kentucky	Spring/Fall	Eastern
Louisiana	Spring	Eastern
Maine	Spring	Eastern
Maryland	Spring/Fall	Eastern
Massachusetts	Spring/Fall	Eastern
Michigan	Spring	Eastern
Minnesota	Spring/Fall	Eastern
Mississippi	Spring/Fall	Eastern
Missouri	Spring/Fall	Eastern

State	Seasons	Subspecies
Montana	Spring/Fall	Merriam's
Nebraska	Spring/Fall	Rio Grande, Merriam's
New Hampshire	Spring/Fall	Eastern
New Jersey	Spring	Eastern
New Mexico	Spring/Fall	Merriam's
New York	Spring/Fall	Eastern
North Carolina	Spring	Eastern
North Dakota	Spring/Fall	Merriam's
Ohio	Spring	Eastern
Oklahoma	Spring/Fall	Rio Grande, Merriam's, Eastern
Oregon	Spring/Fall	Rio Grande, Merriam's
Pennsylvania	Spring/Fall	Eastern
Rhode Island	Spring	Eastern
South Carolina	Spring	Eastern
South Dakota	Spring/Fall	Merriam's
Tennessee	Spring/Fall	Eastern
Texas	Spring/Fall	Rio Grande, Eastern
Utah	Spring	Merriam's
Vermont	Spring/Fall	Eastern
Virginia	Spring/Fall	Eastern
Washington	Spring/Fall	Merriam's
West Virginia	Spring/Fall	Eastern
Wisconsin	Spring/Fall	Eastern
Wyoming	Spring/Fall	Merriam's
Ontario, Canada	Spring only	Eastern

Glossary

Beard. Bristlelike specialized feather tissue hanging from breast of male turkey; also sometimes seen on female.

Blind. A hiding place, natural or man-made, usually camouflaged.

Box call. Call made from solid block of wood or plastic, with paddle rubbed on to make sound.

Brood. The young of a female bird.

Call. The act of reproducing, or the instrument used to reproduce, the sound a turkey makes.

Calling. Imitating the sound of an animal or bird.

Camo. Camouflage.

Choke. Restriction in muzzle of shotgun to concentrate spread of shot.

Cloaca. Common exit of digestive, urinary, and genital tracts.

Corned. Salted.

Cover. Natural hiding place for animals or birds; the act of a male copulating with a female.

Covered. A bred female.

Cricket. Device on arrow to prevent it from going all the way through the turkey.

Crop. First sac of digestive system of bird, a diverticulum of esophagus.

Disk call. Round disk of slate, aluminum, or glass that, when rubbed with a striker, gives off turkey sounds.

Decoy. Model or photograph of live animal or bird used to attract others of the same species.

Driving. A group of hunters proceeding through cover pushing game toward another group.

Drove. Large group of animals, such as cattle or sheep. Sometimes incorrectly used to describe large flocks of turkeys.

Dry pluck. To remove feathers without the use of hot water.

Egg tooth. Tiny hard lump on end of beak of bird prior to hatching, used to break hole in shell.

Flock. Group of birds.

159

Free range. Edible birds, usually chickens or turkeys, allowed to roam on grassy natural areas instead of being confined to small pens.

Freezer burn. Dehydrated areas on frozen food.

Gizzard. Muscular stomach of bird where grinding takes place.

Hang up. When a tom turkey stops and moves back and forth instead of coming toward the caller.

Hard mast. Nuts, particularly acorns, that game feeds on.

Heat. When female of a species is receptive to sexual advances of male. Sometimes referred to as estrus.

Hedgerows. Brushy areas separating fields.

Hen. Female turkey, chicken, or other fowl.

J.A.K.E.S. Juniors Acquiring Knowledge, Ethics, and Sportsmanship — a program of the National Wild Turkey Federation.

Jake. Male turkey under two years of age.

Jerky. Salted, smoked, dried meat that may be kept for some time without refrigeration.

Live oak. Species of oak found in South that stays green year-round.

Mast. Food eaten by bear, deer, and turkeys other than grass, plants, and animals. Usually the fruit, seeds, or nuts of trees and bushes.

Meat pole. Pole between two trees to hang deer carcasses on.

Oil glands. Pair of glands with one opening just ahead of tail on birds.

On stand. Hunter staying in one place watching for game.

Pattern. Design made by shotgun pellets as they hit a large flat target.

Pinfeather. Growing feather emerging from skin still enclosed in its horny sheath.

Pip. Unhatched bird punching hole in shell with its egg tooth.

Pipping. The act of making hole in shell from inside.

Pluck. To remove feathers.

Plunger or push-button box call. Box call that is activated by pushing a plunger instead of scraping with a paddle.

Poult. Young turkey.

Proventriculus. Glandular part of bird's stomach — in turkey just a thickening between crop and gizzard.

Put to bed. Hearing a tom's gobble as he goes to roost in evening.

Roost. Place where birds spend night.

Saltpeter. Potassium nitrate. Gives corned meats their red color; also inhibits bacteria, such as the botulism organism.

Salted. Meat preserved with mixture of salt, sugar, and saltpeter. See *corned.*

Scout. To explore an area to identify game trails, tracks, and other sign, as well as visible game, food and water sources, cover, entrances and exits.

Scrape. Spot where ground has been scraped bare by buck deer during fall rutting season.

Set up. To arrange a place to sit, call, and watch for turkeys.

Setting hen. Female turkey, chicken, or other fowl staying on a nest of eggs to hatch them.

Setup. Location you have set up.

Slate call. Round disk of slate that, when rubbed by a pencil-like piece of plastic, wood, or other material, will give off sound of a turkey.

Snood. Long thin piece of tissue hanging from above beak on a mature tom turkey.

Soft mast. Apples, berries, cherries, and other fruit that serve as seasonal food for game.

Spider. Device to keep arrow from going all the way through a turkey.

Spur. Hornlike pointed projection on legs of mature male turkeys.

Still hunting. To move quietly and slowly, stopping at certain intervals while hunting.

Striker. Pencil-like part of a disk call.

Strut. Stance a tom turkey takes — tail spread, wings down, and body inflated — while trying to impress hens.

Strut zone. Clear area where tom will strut.

Strutting. Act of going into a strut.

Wattle. Massive red tissue around tom turkey's neck.

Wild. Of wild parentage; not confined.

Yolk. Yellow high-protein center of egg.

Yolk reserve. Tiny portion of yolk still remaining in newly hatched turkey poults.

Sources

Magazines

API Outdoors
Field & Stream
Outdoor Life
Shooter's Bible
Turkey Call: The Magazine of the Wild Turkey Federation

Associations

J.A.K.E.S. Program
P. O. Box 530
Edgefield, SC 29824-0530

National Wild Turkey Federation
P. O. Box 530
Edgefield, SC 29824-0530

Suppliers

Cabela's
812 Thirteenth Avenue
Sidney, NE 69160

Classic Game Calls
405 College Drive, Suite 2,
   Department T
Decorah, IA 52101

CVA Black Powder Arm
5988 Peachtree Corners East
Norcross, GA 30071

Dixie Gun Works
P. O. Box 130
Union City, TN 38261

Knight Rifles
234 Airport Road
P. O. Box 130
Centerville, IA 52544

L. L. Bean
386 Main Street
Freeport, ME 04032

LaCrosse Footwear, Inc.
P. O. Box 1328
La Crosse, WI 54602

Orvis
Historic Route 7A
Manchester, VT 05254-0798

Perfection Diaphragm Turkey
   Calls, Inc.
P. O. Box 164
Stephenson, VA 22656

Quaker Boy
5455 Webster Road
Orchard Park, NY 14127

Skeeter Dodd
P. O. Box 110892
Nashville, TN 37222

Thompson Center
Farmington Road
P. O. Box 5002
Rochester, NH 03867

Walls Industries Inc.
P. O. Box 98
Cleburne, TX 76031

Index

Page references in *italics* indicate illustrations; **bold** indicates charts.

Other Storey Titles
You Will Enjoy

Basic Butchering of Livestock & Game, by John J. Mettler. A book for anyone who hunts, farms, or buys large quantities of meat, it takes the mystery out of slaughtering and butchering everything from beef and veal, to venison and pork. 208 pages. Paperback. ISBN 0-88266-391-7.

Raising Your Own Turkeys, by Leonard S. Mercia. This book offers complete, up-to-date, how-to information on raising turkeys, from young poults to delicious, thick-breasted birds. 144 pages. Paperback. ISBN 0-88266-253-8.

Tan Your Hide! Home Tanning Leathers & Furs, by Phyllis Hobson. Complete with photographs and line drawings, this book explains what you need to tan your own leather and fur, and all the steps in doing it right. 144 pages. Paperback. ISBN 0-88266-101-9.

Keeping a Nature Journal, by Clare Walker Leslie and Charles E. Roth. Filled with examples, exercises, and inspiring suggestions, this book encourages people to become more in touch with nature and better observers by keeping a journal. The authors provide detailed step-by-step instructions on how to start, maintain, and continually build upon and experiment with keeping a nature journal. 192 pages. Paperback. ISBN 1-58017-306-3.

The Backyard Bird-Lover's Guide, by Jan Mahnken. Covers feeding, territory, courtship, nesting, laying, and parenting characteristics of many birds. Identification section describes 135 species and includes watercolors by Jeffrey C. Domm. 320 pages. Paperback. ISBN 0-88266-927-3. Hardcover. ISBN 1-58017-088-9.

Birdfeeders, Shelters & Baths: Over 25 Complete Step-by-Step Projects for the Weekend Woodworker, by Edward A. Baldwin. Designs for a wide range of birdfeeders and baths that will attract birds to your backyard all year. 128 pages. Paperback. ISBN 0-88266-623-1.

These books and other Storey books are available at your bookstore, farm store, garden center, or directly from Storey Publishing, 210 MASS MoCA Way, North Adams, MA 01247, or by calling 1-800-441-5700. Visit our Web site at www.storey.com.